HOW TO SING

HOW TO SING

[MEINE GESANGSKUNST]

BY

LILLI LEHMANN

TRANSLATED FROM THE GERMAN

BY

RICHARD ALDRICH

Publishers/WHITEHALL COMPANY

601 Skokie Blvd./Northbrook, Ill. 60062

Publishers/WHITEHALL COMPANY

601 Skokie Blvd./Northbrook, Ill. 60062

Manufactured in the United States of America

ISBN (paper) 0-87655-530-X

CONTENTS

CONTENTS

CONTENTS

SECTION XVIII

CONTENTS

SECTION XXXVII

SECTION XXXVIII

SECTION XXXIX

MY PURPOSE

My purpose is to discuss simply, intelligibly, yet from a scientific point of view, the sensations known to us in singing, and exactly ascertained in my experience, by the expressions "singing open," "covered," "dark," "nasal," "in the head," or "in the neck," "forward," or "back." These expressions correspond to our sensations in singing; but they are unintelligible as long as the causes of those sensations are unknown, and everybody has a different idea of them. Many singers try their whole lives long to produce them and never succeed. This happens because science understands too little of singing, the singer too little of science. I mean that the physiological explanations of the highly complicated processes of singing are not plainly enough put for the singer, who has to concern himself chiefly with his sensations in singing and guide himself by them.   Scientific men are not at all agreed as to the exact functions of the several organs; the humblest singer knows something about them. Every serious artist has a sincere desire to help others reach the goal — the goal toward which all singers are striving: to sing well and beautifully.

The true art of song has always been possessed and will always be possessed by such individuals as are dowered by nature with all that is needful for it — that is, healthy vocal organs, uninjured by vicious habits of speech; a good ear, a talent for singing, intelligence, industry, and energy.

In former times eight years were devoted to the study of singing — at the Prague Conservatory, for instance.   Most of the mistakes and misunderstandings of the pupil could be discovered before he secured an engagement, and the teacher could spend so much time in correcting them that the pupil learned to pass judgment on himself properly.

But art to-day must be pursued like everything else, by steam. Artists are turned out in factories, that is, in so-called conservatories, or by teachers who give lessons ten or twelve hours a day. In two years they receive a certificate of competence, or at least the diploma of the factory. The latter, especially, I consider a crime, that the state should prohibit.

All the inflexibility and unskilfulness, mistakes and deficiencies, which were formerly disclosed during a long course of study, do not appear now, under the factory system, until the student's public career has begun. There can be no question of correcting them, for there is no time, no teacher, no critic; and the executant has learned nothing, absolutely nothing, whereby he could undertake to distinguish or correct them.

The incompetence and lack of talent whitewashed over by the factory concern lose only too soon their plausible brilliancy. A failure in life is generally the sad end of such a factory product; and to factory methods the whole art of song is more and more given over as a sacrifice.

I cannot stand by and see these things with indifference. My artistic conscience urges me to disclose all that I have learned and that has become clear to me in the course of my career, for the benefit of art; and to give up my "secrets," which seem to be secrets only because students so rarely pursue the path of proper study to its end. If artists, often such only in name, come to a realization of their deficiencies, they lack only too frequently the courage to acknowledge them to others. Not until we artists all reach the point when we can take counsel with each other about our mistakes and deficiencies, and discuss the means for overcoming them, putting our pride in our pockets, will bad singing and inartistic effort be checked, and our noble art of singing come into its rights again.

MY TITLE TO WRITE ON THE ART OF SONG

Rarely are so many desirable and necessary antecedents united as in my case.

The child of two singers, my mother being gifted musically quite out of the common, and active for many years not only as a dramatic singer, but also as a harp virtuoso, I, with my sister Marie, received a very careful musical education; and later a notable course of instruction in singing from her. From my fifth year on I listened daily to singing lessons; from my ninth year I played accompaniments on the pianoforte, sang all the missing parts, in French, Italian, German, and Bohemian; got thoroughly familiar with all the operas, and very soon knew how to tell good singing from bad. Our mother took care, too, that we should hear all the visiting notabilities of that time in opera as well as in concert; and there were many of them every year at the Deutsches Landestheater in Prague.

She herself had found a remarkable singing teacher in the Frankfort basso, Föppel; and kept her voice noble, beautiful, young, and strong to the end of her life, — that is, till her seventy-seventh year, — notwithstanding enormous demands upon it and many a blow of fate. She could diagnose a voice infallibly; but required a probation of three to four months to test talent and power of making progress.

I have been on the stage since my eighteenth year; that is, for thirty-four years. In Prague I took part every day in operas, operettas, plays, and farces. Thereafter in Danzig I sang from eighteen to twenty times a month in coloratura and soubrette parts; also in Leipzig, and later, fifteen years in Berlin. In addition I sang in very many oratorios and concerts, and gave lessons now and then.

As long as my mother lived she was my severest critic, never satisfied. Finally I became such for myself. Now fifteen years more have passed, of which I spent eight very exacting ones as a dramatic singer in America, afterward fulfilling engagements as a star, in all languages, in Germany, Austria, Hungary, France, England, and Sweden. My study of singing, nevertheless, was not relaxed. I kept it up more and more zealously by myself, learned something from everybody, learned to *hear* myself and others.

For many years I have been devoting myself to the important questions relating to singing, and believe that I have finally found what I have been seeking. It has been my endeavor to set down as clearly as possible all that I have learned through zealous, conscientious study by myself and with others, and thereby to offer to my colleagues something that will bring order into the chaos of their methods of singing; something based on science as well as on sensations in singing; something that will bring expressions often misunderstood into clear relation with the exact functions of the vocal organs.

In what I have just said I wish to give a sketch of my career only to show what my voice has endured, and why, notwithstanding the enormous demands I have made upon it, it has lasted so well. One who has sung for a short time, and then has lost his voice, and for this reason becomes a singing teacher, has never sung consciously; it has simply been an accident, and this accident will be repeated, for good or for ill, in his pupils.

The talent in which all the requirements of an artist are united is very rare. Real talent will get along, even with an inferior teacher, in some way or another; while the best teacher cannot produce talent where there is none. Such a teacher, however, will not beguile people with promises that cannot be kept.

My chief attention I devote to artists, whom I can, perhaps, assist in their difficult, but glorious, profession. One is never done with learning; and that is especially true of singers. I earnestly hope that I may

leave them something, in my researches, ex-
periences, and studies, that will be of use. I
regard it as my duty; and I confide it to all
who are striving earnestly for improvement.

GRÜNEWALD, Oct. 31, 1900.

SECTION I

PRELIMINARY PRACTICE

IT is very important for all who wish to become artists to begin their work not with practical exercises in singing, but with serious practice in tone production, in breathing in and out, in the functions of the lungs and palate, in clear pronunciation of all letters, and with speech in general.

Then it would soon be easy to recognize talent or the lack of it. Many would open their eyes in wonder over the difficulties of learning to sing, and the proletariat of singers would gradually disappear. With them would go the singing conservatories and the bad teachers who, for a living, teach everybody that comes, and promise to make everybody a great artist.

Once when I was acting as substitute for a teacher in a conservatory, the best pupils of the institution were promised me,— those who needed only the finishing touches. But when, after my first lesson, I went to the director and complained of the ignorance of the pupils, my mouth was closed with these words, "For Heaven's sake, don't say such things, or we could never keep our conservatory going!"

I had enough, and went.

The best way is for pupils to learn preparatory books by heart, and make drawings. In this way they will get the best idea of the vocal organs, and learn their functions by sensation as soon as they begin to sing. The pupil should be subjected to strict examinations.

In what does artistic singing differ from natural singing?

In a clear understanding of all the organs concerned in voice production, and their functions, singly and together; in the understanding of the sensations in singing, conscientiously studied and scientifically explained; in a gradually cultivated power of contracting and relaxing the muscles of the vocal organs, that power culminating in the ability to submit them to severe exertions and keep them under control. The prescribed tasks must be mastered so that they can be done without exertion, with the whole heart and soul, and with complete understanding.

How is this to be attained?

Through natural gifts, among which I reckon the possession of sound organs and a well-favored body; through study guided by an excellent teacher *who can sing well himself*, — study that must be kept up for at least six years, without counting the preliminary work.

Only singers formed on such a basis, after years of work, deserve the title of artist; only such have a right to look forward to a lasting future, and only those equipped with such a knowledge ought to teach.

Of what consists artistic singing?

Of a clear understanding, first and foremost, of breathing, in and out; of an understanding of the form through which the breath has to flow, prepared by a proper position of the larynx, the tongue, and the palate. Of a knowledge and understanding of the functions of the muscles of the abdomen and diaphragm, which regulate the breath pressure; then, of the chest-muscle tension, against which the breath is forced, and whence, under the control of the singer, after passing through the vocal cords, it beats against the resonating surfaces and vibrates in the cavities of the head. Of a highly cultivated skill and flexibility in adjusting all the vocal organs and in putting them into minutely graduated movements, without inducing changes through the pronunciation of words or the execution of musical figures that shall be injurious to the tonal beauty or the artistic expression of the song. Of an immense muscular power in the breathing apparatus and all the vocal organs, the strengthening of which to endure sustained exertion cannot be begun too long in advance; and the exercising of which, as long as one sings in public, must never be remitted for a single day.

As beauty and stability of tone do not depend upon excessive *pressure* of the breath, so the muscular power of the organs used in singing does not depend on convulsive rigidity, but in that snakelike power of contracting and loosening,[1] which a singer must consciously have under perfect control.

The study needed for this occupies an entire lifetime; not only because the singer must perfect himself more and more in the

---

[1] In physiology when the muscles resume their normal state, they are said to be *relaxed*. But as I wish to avoid giving a false conception in our vocal sensations, I prefer to use the word " loosening."

rôles of his repertory — even after he has
been performing them year in and year out,
— but because he must continually strive for
progress, setting himself tasks that require
greater and greater mastery and strength,
and thereby demand fresh study.

He who stands still, goes backward.

Nevertheless, there are fortunately gifted
geniuses in whom are already united all the
qualities needed to attain greatness and perfection, and whose circumstances in life are
equally fortunate; who can reach the goal
earlier, without devoting their whole lives
to it. Thus, for instance, in Adelina Patti
everything was united, — the splendid voice,
paired with great talent for singing, and the
long oversight of her studies by her distinguished teacher, Strakosch. She never sang
rôles that did not suit her voice; in her
earlier years she sang only arias and duets or
single solos, never taking part in ensembles.
She never sang even her limited repertory

when she was indisposed. She never attended rehearsals, but came to the theatre in the evening and sang triumphantly, without ever having seen the persons who sang and acted with her. She spared herself rehearsals which, on the day of the performance, or the day before, exhaust all singers, because of the excitement of all kinds attending them, and which contribute neither to the freshness of the voice nor to the joy of the profession.

Although she was a Spaniard by birth and an American by early adoption, she was, so to speak, the greatest Italian singer of my time. All was absolutely good, correct, and flawless, the voice like a bell that you seemed to hear long after its singing had ceased.

Yet she could give no explanation of her art, and answered all her colleagues' questions concerning it with an " Ah, je n'en sais rien ! "

She possessed, unconsciously, as a gift of

c

nature, a union of all those qualities that all other singers must attain and possess *consciously*. Her vocal organs stood in the most favorable relations to each other. Her talent, and her remarkably trained ear, maintained control over the beauty of her singing and of her voice. The fortunate circumstances of her life preserved her from all injury. The purity and flawlessness of her tone, the beautiful equalization of her whole voice, constituted the magic by which she held her listeners entranced. Moreover, she was beautiful and gracious in appearance.

The accent of great dramatic power she did not possess; yet I ascribe this more to her intellectual indolence than to her lack of ability.

SECTION II

OF THE BREATH

THE breath becomes voice through the operation of the will, and the instrumentality of the vocal organs.

To regulate the breath, to prepare a passage of the proper form through which it shall flow, circulate, develop itself, and reach the necessary resonating chambers, must be our chief task.

Concerning the breath and much more besides there is so much that is excellent in Oscar Guttmann's "Gymnastik der Stimme" that I can do no better than to refer to it and recommend it strongly to the attention of all earnest students.

How do I breathe?

Very short of breath by nature, my mother had to keep me as a little child almost sitting upright in bed. After I had outgrown that and as a big girl could run around and play well enough, I still had much trouble with shortness of breath in the beginning of my singing lessons. For years I practised breathing exercises every day without singing, and still do so with especial pleasure, now that everything that relates to the breath and the voice has become clear to me. Soon I had got so far that I could hold a swelling and diminishing tone from fifteen to eighteen seconds.

I had learned this: to draw in the abdomen and diaphragm, raise the chest and hold the breath in it by the aid of the ribs; in letting out the breath *gradually* to relax the body and to let the chest fall slowly. To do everything *thoroughly* I doubtless exaggerated it all. But since for twenty-five years I have breathed in this way almost exclusively, with the utmost care, I have naturally attained great dexterity in it; and my abdominal and chest muscles and my diaphragm have been strengthened to a re-markable degree. Yet I was not satisfied.

A horn player in Berlin with the power of holding a very long breath, once told me in answer to a question, that he drew in his abdomen and diaphragm very strongly, but immediately relaxed his abdomen again as soon as he began to play. I tried the same thing with the *best results*. Quite different, and very naïve, was the answer I once got from three German orchestral horn players in America. They looked at me in entire be-wilderment, and appeared not to understand in the least my questions as to how they breathed. Two of them declared that the best way was not to think about it at all. But when I asked if their teachers had never told them how they should breathe, the third answered, after some reflection, " Oh, yes! " and pointed in a general way to his stomach. The first two were right, in so far as too violent inhalation of breath is really unde-sirable, because thereby *too much* air is drawn

in. But such ignorance of the subject is dis-
heartening, and speaks ill for the conservatories in which the players were trained,
whose performances naturally are likely to
give art a black eye.

Undoubtedly I took in too much air in
breathing, and thereby stiffened various organs, depriving my muscles of their elasticity.
Yet, with all my care and preparation, I
often, when I had not given special thought
to it, had too little breath, rather than too
much. I felt, too, after excessive inhalation,
as if I must emit a certain amount of air before I began to sing. Finally I abandoned
all superfluous drawing in of the abdomen
and diaphragm, inhaled but little, and began
to pay special attention to emitting the
smallest possible amount of breath, which I
found very serviceable.

How do I breathe now?

My diaphragm I scarcely draw in consciously, my abdomen never; I feel the

breath fill my lungs, and my upper ribs expand. Without raising my chest especially high, I force the breath against it, and hold it fast there. At the same time I raise my palate high and prevent the escape of breath through the nose. The diaphragm beneath reacts against it, and furnishes pressure from the abdomen. Chest, diaphragm, the closed epiglottis, and the raised palate all form a supply chamber for the breath.

Only in this way is the breath under the control of the singer, through the pressure against the chest tension muscles. (*This is very important.*) From now on the breath must be emitted from the supply chamber very sparingly, but with unceasing uniformity and strength, without once being held back, to the vocal cords, which will further regulate it as far as possible. The more directly the breath pressure is exerted against the chest, — one has the feeling, in this, of singing the tone against the chest whence it must be *pressed* out, — the less breath flows through the vocal cords, and the less, consequently, are these overburdened.

In this way, under control, in the passage formed for it above the tongue by that organ, it reaches the resonance chambers prepared for it by the raising and lowering of the soft palate, and those in the cavities of the head. Here it forms whirling currents of tone; these now must circulate uninterrupted for as long as possible and fill all the accessible resonating surfaces, which must be maintained in an elastic state. This is necessary to bring the tone to its perfect purity. Not till these currents have been sufficiently used up and passed through the " bell," or cup-shaped resonating cavity, of the mouth and lips, may it be allowed to stream from the mouth unimpeded. Yet the *sensation* must be as if the breath were constantly escaping from the mouth.

To observe and keep under control these many functions, singly or in conjunction, forms the ceaseless delight of the never failing fountain of song study.

Thus, in shaping the passage for the breath, the larynx, tongue, and palate, which can be placed at will, are employed. The vocal cords, which can best be imagined as inner lips, we have under control neither as beginners nor as artists. *We do not feel them.* We first become conscious of them through the controlling apparatus of the breath, which teaches us to *spare* them, by emitting breath through them in the least possible quantity and of even pressure, whereby a steady tone can be produced. I even maintain that all is won, when — as Victor Maurel says — we regard them directly as the breath regulators, and relieve them of all overwork through the controlling apparatus of the chest-muscle tension.

Through the form prepared by the larynx, tongue, and palate, we can direct the breath, previously under control and regulation, toward the particular resonating surfaces on the palate, or in the cavities of the head,

which are suitable to each tone.   This rule
remains the same for all voices.

As soon as the breath leaves the larynx,
it is divided. (Previously, in inhalation, a
similar thing happens; but this does not
concern us immediately, and I prefer to direct
the singer's chief attention to the second oc-
currence.)   One part may press toward the
palate, the other toward the cavities of the
head. The division of the breath occurs
regularly, from the deepest bass to the
highest tenor or soprano, step for step, vibration for vibration, without regard to sex or
individuality.   Only the differing size or
strength of the vocal organs through which
the breath flows, the breathing apparatus, or
the skill with which they are used, are different in different individuals.   The seat of
the breath, the law of its division, as well
as the resonating surfaces, are always the
same and are differentiated at most through
difference of habit.

SECTION III

OF THE BREATH AND WHIRLING CURRENTS
(SINGING FORWARD)

THE veriest beginner knows that in order
to use the breath to the fullest advantage,
it must remain very long diffused back in
the mouth. A mistaken idea of "singing
forward" misleads most to *press* it forward
and thus allow it to be speedily dissipated.

The column of breath coming in an uninterrupted stream from the larynx, must, as
soon as it flows into the form prepared for
it according to the required tone, by the
tongue and palate, fill this form, soaring
through all its corners, with its vibrations.
It makes whirling currents, which circulate
in the elastic form surrounding it, and it
must remain there till the tone is high
enough, strong enough, and sustained enough

27

to satisfy the judgment of the singer as well as the ear of the listener. Should there be lacking the least element of pitch, strength, or duration, the tone is imperfect and does not meet the requirement.

Learning and teaching to hear is the first task of both pupil and teacher. One is impossible without the other. It is the most difficult as well as the most grateful task, and it is the only way to reach perfection.

Even if the pupil unconsciously should produce a flawless tone, it is the teacher's duty to acquaint him clearly with the *causes* of it. It is not enough to sing well; one must also know how one does it. The teacher must tell the pupil constantly, making him describe clearly his sensations in singing, and understand fully the physiological factors that coöperate to produce them.

The sensations in singing must coincide with mine as here described, if they are to be considered as correct; for mine are based logically on physiological causes and correspond precisely with the operation of these causes. Moreover, all my pupils tell me — often, to be sure, not till many months have passed — how exact my explanations are; how accurately, on the strength of them, they have learned to feel the physiological processes. They have learned, slowly, to be sure, to become conscious of their errors and false impressions; for it is very difficult to ascertain such mistakes and false adjustments of the organs. False sensations in singing and disregarded or false ideas of physiological processes cannot immediately be stamped out. A long time is needed for the mind to be able to form a clear image of those processes, and not till then can knowledge and improvement be expected. The teacher must repeatedly explain the physiological processes, the pupil repeatedly disclose every confusion and uncertainty he feels, until the perfect consciousness of his sensations in singing is irrevocably impressed upon his memory, that is, has become a habit.

Among a hundred singers hardly one can be found whose single tones meet every requirement. And among a thousand listeners, even among teachers, and among artists, hardly one hears it.

I admit that such perfect tones sometimes, generally quite unconsciously, are heard from young singers, and especially from beginners, and never fail to make an impression. The teacher hears that they are good, so does the public. Only a very few know why, even among singers, because only a very few know the laws governing perfect tone production. Their talent, their ear perchance, tell them the truth; but the causes they neither know nor look for.

On such "unconscious singing" directors, managers, and even conductors, build mistakenly their greatest hopes. No one hears what is lacking, or what will soon be lacking, and all are surprised when experienced singers protest against it.

They become enthusiastic, properly, over beautiful voices, but pursue quite the wrong path in training them for greater tasks. As soon as such persons are obtained, they are immediately bundled into *all* rôles; they have hardly time to learn one rôle by heart, to say nothing of comprehending it and working it up artistically. The stars must shine *immediately!* But with what resources? With the fresh voice alone? Who is there to teach them to use their resources on the stage? Who to husband them for the future? The manager? the director? Not at all. When the day comes that they can no longer perform what, not they themselves, but the directors, expected of them, they are put to one side, and if they do not possess great energy and strength, often entirely succumb. They could not meet the demands made upon them, because they did not know how to use their resources.

I shall be told that tones well sung, even unconsciously, are enough. But that is not true. The least unfavorable circumstance, overexertion, indisposition, an unaccustomed situation, anything can blow out the "unconscious" one's light, or at least make it flicker badly. Of any self-help, when there is ignorance of all the fundamentals, there can be no question. Any help is grasped at. Then appears the so-called (but false) "individuality," under whose mask so much that is bad presents itself to art and before the public.

This is not remarkable, in view of the complexity of the phenomena of song. Few teachers concern themselves with the fundamental studies; they often do not sing at all themselves, or they sing quite wrongly; and consequently can neither describe the vocal sensations nor test them in others. Theory alone is of no value whatever. With old singers the case is often quite the contrary — so both seize whatever help they can lay hold of. The breath, that vibrates against the soft palate, when it is raised, or behind it in the cavities of the head, produces whirling currents through its continuous streaming forth and its twofold division. These currents can circulate only in unbroken completeness of form. The longer their form remains unimpaired, and the more economically the continuous breath pressure is maintained, the less breath do these currents need, the less is emitted unused from the mouth.

If an elastic form is found in the mouth in which the currents can circulate untouched by any pressure or undue contraction or expansion of it, the breath becomes practically unlimited. That is the simple solution of the paradox that without deep breathing one may often have much breath, and, after elaborate preparations, often none at all; because the chief attention is generally directed to inhalation, instead of to the elastic forming of the organs for the breath, sound currents, and tone. The one thing needed is the knowledge of the causes, and the necessary skill in pre-

D

paring the form, avoiding all pressure that could injure it, whether originating in the larynx, tongue, or palate, or in the organs that furnish the breath pressure.

The singer's endeavors, consequently, must be directed to keeping the breath as long as possible sounding and vibrating not only forward but back in the mouth, since the resonance of the tone is spread upon and above the entire palate, extends from the front teeth to the wall of the throat. He must concern himself with preparing for the vibrations, pliantly and with mobility, a powerful, elastic, almost floating envelope, which must be filled entirely, with the help of a continuous vocal mixture, — a mixture of which the components are indistinguishable.

SECTION IV

THE SINGER'S PHYSIOLOGICAL STUDIES

SCIENCE has explained all the processes of
the vocal organs in their chief functions, and
many methods of singing have been based
upon physiology, physics, and phonetics. To
a certain extent scientific explanations are
absolutely necessary for the singer — as long
as they are confined to the sensations in singing, foster understanding of the phenomenon,
and summon up an intelligible picture. This
is what uninterpreted sensations in singing
cannot do; of which fact the clearest demon-
stration is given by the expressions, "bright,"
"dark," "nasal," "singing forward," etc., that
I began by mentioning and that are almost
always falsely understood. They are quite
meaningless without the practical teachings
of the sensations of such singers as have di-

rected their attention to them with a knowledge of the end in view, and are competent to correlate them with the facts of science.

The singer is usually worried by the word "physiology"; but only because he does not clearly understand the limits of its teachings. The singer need, will, and must, know a little of it. We learn so much that is useless in this life, why not learn that which is of the utmost service to us? What, in brief, does it mean? Perfect consciousness in moving the vocal organs, and through the aid of the ear, in placing them at will in certain relations with each other; the fact that the soft palate can be drawn up against the hard palate; that the tongue is able to take many different positions, and that the larynx, by the assistance of the vocal sound oo, takes a low position, and by that of the vowel ā a high one; that all muscles contract in activity and in normal inactivity are relaxed; that we must strengthen them by continued vocal gymnastics so that they may be able to sus-

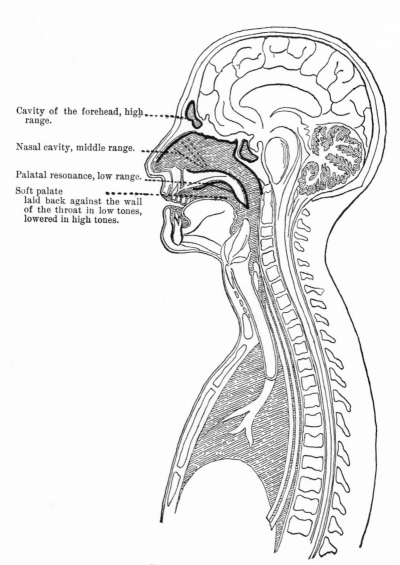

Cavity of the forehead, high range.

Nasal cavity, middle range.

Palatal resonance, low range.

Soft palate
laid back against the wall
of the throat in low tones,
lowered in high tones.

lines denote the resonance

tain long-continued exertion; and must keep them elastic and use them so. It includes also the well-controlled activity of diaphragm, chest, neck, and face muscles. This is all that physiology means for the vocal organs. Since these things all operate together, one without the others can accomplish nothing; if the least is lacking, singing is quite impossible, or is entirely bad.

Physiology is concerned also with muscles, nerves, sinews, ligaments, and cartilage, all of which are used in singing, but all of which we cannot feel. We cannot even feel the vocal cords. Certainly much depends for the singer upon their proper condition; and whether as voice producers or breath regulators, we all have good reason always to spare them as much as possible, and never to overburden them.

Though we cannot feel the vocal cords, we can, nevertheless, hear, by observing whether the tone is even, — in the emission of the breath under control, — whether they are per-

forming their functions properly. Overburdening them through pressure, or emitting of
the breath without control, results in weaken-
ing them. The irritation of severe coughing,
thoughtless talking or shouting immediately
after singing may also set up serious congestion of the vocal cords, which can be reme-
died only through slow gymnastics of the
tongue and laryngeal muscles, by the pronunciation of vowels in conjunction with
consonants. Inactivity of the vocal organs
will not cure it, or perhaps not till after the
lapse of years.

A good singer can *never* lose his voice.
Mental agitation or severe colds can for a
time deprive the singer of the use of his vocal
organs, or seriously impair them. Only those
who have been singing without consciously
correct use of their organs can become dis-
heartened over it; those who know better
will, with more or less difficulty, cure themselves, and by the use of vocal gymnastics
bring their vocal organs into condition again.

For this reason, if for no other, singers should seek to acquire accurate knowledge of their own organs, as well as of their functions, that they may not let themselves be burnt, cut, and cauterized by unscrupulous physicians. Leave the larynx and all connected with it alone; strengthen the organs by daily vocal gymnastics and a healthy, *sober* mode of life; beware of catching cold after singing; do not sit and talk in restaurants.

Students of singing should use the early morning hours, and fill their days with the various branches of their study. Sing every day only so much, that on the next day you can practise again, feeling fresh and ready for work, as *regular* study requires. Better one hour every day than ten to-day and none to-morrow.

The public singer should also do his practising early in the day, that he may have himself well in hand by evening. How often one feels indisposed in the morning! Any physical reason is sufficient to make singing difficult, or even impossible; it need not be connected necessarily with the vocal organs; in fact, I believe it very rarely is. For this reason, in two hours everything may have changed.

I remember a charming incident in New York. Albert Niemann, our heroic tenor, who was to sing *Lohengrin* in the evening, complained to me in the morning of severe hoarseness. To give up a rôle in America costs the singer, as well as the director, much money. My advice was to wait.

Niemann. What do you do, then, when you are hoarse?

I. Oh, I practise and see whether it still troubles me.

Niem. Indeed; and what do you practise?

I. Long, slow scales.

Niem. Even if you are hoarse?

I. Yes; if I want to sing, or have to, I try it.

Niem. Well, what are they? Show me.

The great scale, the infallible cure.

I showed them to him; he sang them, with words of abuse in the meantime; but gradually his hoarseness grew better. He did not send word of his inability to appear in the evening, but sang, and better than ever, with enormous success.

I myself had to sing *Norma* in Vienna some years ago, and got up in the morning quite hoarse. By nine o'clock I tried my infallible remedy, but could not sing above A flat, though in the evening I should have to reach high D flat and E flat. I was on the point of giving up, because the case seemed to me so desperate. Nevertheless, I practised till eleven o'clock, half an hour at a time, and noticed that I was gradually getting better. In the evening I had my D flat and E flat at my command and was in brilliant form. People said they had seldom heard me sing so well.

I could give numberless instances, all going to show that you never can tell early in the day how you are going to feel in the evening. I much prefer, for instance, not to feel so very well early in the day, because it may easily happen that the opposite may be the case later on, which is much less agreeable. If you wish to sing only when you are in good form, you must excuse yourself ninety-nine times out of a hundred. You must learn to know your own vocal organs thoroughly and be able to sing; must do everything that is calculated to keep you in good condition. This includes chiefly rest for the nerves, care of the body, and gymnastics of the voice, that you may be able to defy all possible chances.

Before all, never neglect to practise every morning, regularly, proper singing exercises through the whole compass of the voice. Do it with *painful* seriousness; and never think that vocal gymnastics weary the singer. On the contrary, they bring refreshment and power of endurance to him who will become master of his vocal organs.

SECTION V

THROUGH the lowering of the pillars of the fauces, which is the same as raising the soft palate, the outflowing breath is divided into two parts.

I have sketched the following representation of it: —

Division of the breath.

By raising the pillars of the fauces, which closes off the throat from the cavities of the head, the chest voice is produced; that is, the lowest range of all kinds of voices. This occurs when the main stream of breath, spreading over against the high-arched palate, completely utilizes all its resonating surfaces. This is the palatal resonance, in which there is the most power (Plate A).

When the soft palate is raised high behind

45

the nose, the pillars of the fauces are lowered, and this frees the way for the main stream of breath to the head cavities. This now is poured out, filling the nose, forehead, and head cavities. This makes the head tone. Called head tone in women, falsetto in men, it is the highest range of all classes of voices, the resonance of the head cavities (Plate C).

Between these two extreme functions of the palate and breath, one stream of breath gives some of its force to the other; and when equally divided they form the medium range of all classes of voices (Plate B).

The singer must always have in his mind's eye a picture of this divided stream of breath.

As I have already said, in the lowest tones of all voices the main stream of breath is projected against the palate; the pillars of the fauces, being stretched to their fullest extent, and drawn back to the wall of the throat, allow *almost* no breath to reach the head cavities.

I say *almost* none, for, as a matter of fact,

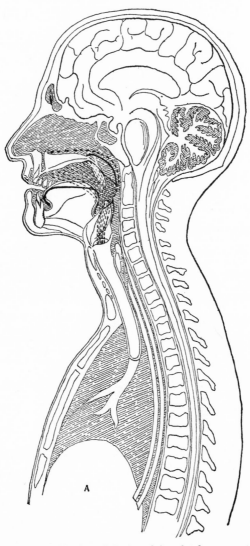

lines denote division of the breath in palatal resonance, lower
range of male and female voices

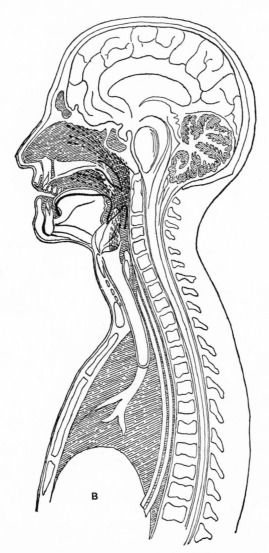

lines denote division of the breath in the middle range

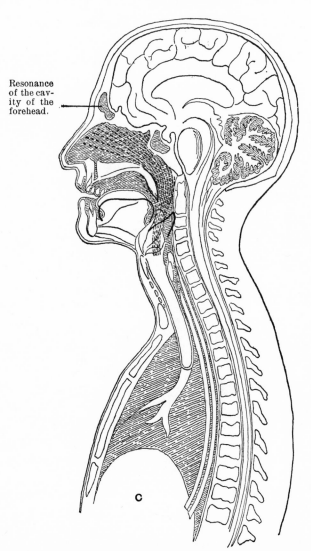

Resonance
of the cav-
ity of the
forehead.

C

lines denote division of the breath in the resonance of the head
cavity, high range

a branch stream of breath, however small,
must be forced back, behind and above the
pillars, first into the nose, later into the
forehead and the cavities of the head. This
forms the overtones (head tones) which must
vibrate with all tones, even the lowest. These
overtones lead over from the purest chest
tones, slowly, with a constantly changing
mixture of both kinds of resonance, first to
the high tones of bass and baritone, the low
tones of tenor, the middle tones of alto and
soprano, finally, to the purest head tones, the
highest tones of the tenor-falsetto or soprano.
(See the plates.)

The extremely delicate gradation of the
scale of increase of the resonance of the head
cavities in ascending passages, and of increase
of palatal resonance in descending, depends
upon the skill to make the palate act elastically, and to let the breath, under control of
the abdominal and chest pressure, flow uninterruptedly in a gentle stream into the resonating chambers. Through the previous

preparation of the larynx and tongue, it must reach its resonating surfaces as though passing through a cylinder, and must circulate in the form previously prepared for it, proper for each tone and vowel sound. This form surrounds it gently but firmly. The supply of air remains continuously the same, *rather increasing than diminishing,* notwithstanding the fact that the quantity which the abdominal pressure has furnished the vocal cords from the supply chamber is a very small one. That it may not hinder further progression, the form must remain elastic and sensitive to the most delicate modification of the vowel sound. If the tone is to have life, it must always be able to conform to any vowel sound. The least displacement of the form or interruption of the breath breaks up the whirling currents and vibrations, and consequently affects the tone, its vibrancy, its strength, and its duration.

In singing a continuous passage upward, the form becomes higher and more pliant; the

most pliable place on the palate is drawn upward.   (See Plate A.)

When I sing a single tone I can give it
much more power, much more palatal or
nasal resonance, than I could give in a
series of ascending tones.   In a musical figure
I must attack the lowest note in such a way
that I can easily reach the highest.   I must,
therefore, give it much more head tone than
the single tone requires.   (Very important.)
When advancing farther, I have the feeling
on the palate, above and behind the nose,
toward the cavities of the head, of a strong
but very elastic rubber ball, which I fill like a
balloon with my breath streaming up far back
of it.   And this filling keeps on in even meas-
ure.   That is, the branch stream of the breath,
which flows into the head cavities, must be
free to flow very strongly without hindrance.
(See Plate B.)

I can increase the size of this ball above,
to a pear shape, as soon as I think of singing
higher ; and, indeed, I heighten the form

before I go on from the tone just sung, making it, so to speak, *higher* in that way, and thus keep the form, that is, the " propagation form," ready for the next higher tone, which I can now reach easily, as long as no interruption in the stream of breath against the mucous membrane can take place. For this reason the breath must *never be held back*, but must always be emitted in a more and more powerful stream. The higher the tone, the more numerous are the vibrations, the more rapidly the whirling currents circulate, and the more unchangeable must the form be.

Catarrh often dries up the mucous membrane; then the tones are inclined to break off. At such times one must sing with peculiar circumspection, and with an especially powerful stream of breath behind the tone: it is better to take breath frequently. In a descending scale or figure I must, on the contrary, preserve very carefully the form taken for the highest tone. I must not go higher, nor yet, under any circumstances, lower, but

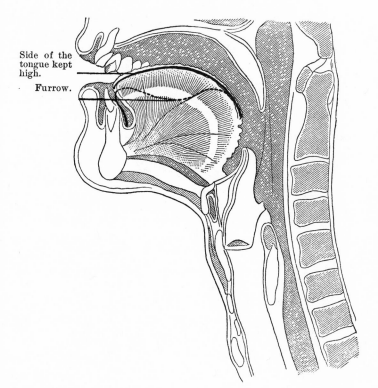

Side of the
tongue kept
high.

Furrow.

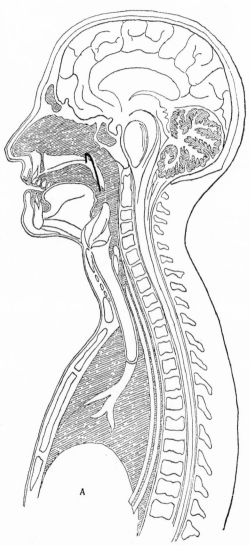

A

line denotes:
Sensation in raising the soft palate for high notes.
Sensation of the form in rapid upward passages.
Division of the breath favors the resonance of head cavities.

must imagine that I remain at the same pitch, and must suggest to myself that I am striking the same tone again. The form may gradu ally be a little modified at the upper end that is, the soft palate is lowered very carefully behind the nose: keeping almost always to the form employed for the highest tone, sing the figure to its end, toward the nose, with the help of the vowel *oo*. (This auxiliary vowel *oo* means nothing more than that the larynx is slowly lowered in position.)

When this happens, the resonance of the head cavities is diminished, that of the palate increased; for the soft palate sinks, and the pillars of the fauces are raised more and more. Yet the head tone must not be entirely free from palatal resonance. Both remain to the last breath united, mutually supporting each other in ascending and descending passages, and alternately but inaudibly increasing and diminishing.

These things go to make up the form: —

The raising and lowering of the soft palate, and the corresponding lowering and raising of the pillars of the fauces.

The proper position of the tongue: the tip rests on the lower front teeth — mine even as low as the roots of the teeth.

The back of the tongue must stand high and free from the throat, ready for any movement. A furrow must be formed in the tongue, which is least prominent in the lowest tones, and in direct head tones may even completely disappear. As soon as the tone demands the palatal resonance, the furrow must be made prominent and kept so. In my case it can always be seen. This is one of the most important matters, upon which too much emphasis can hardly be laid. As soon as the furrow in the tongue shows itself, the tone must sound right; for then the mass of the tongue is kept away from the throat, and, since its sides are raised, it is kept out of the way of the tone.

It lies flattest in the lowest tones because

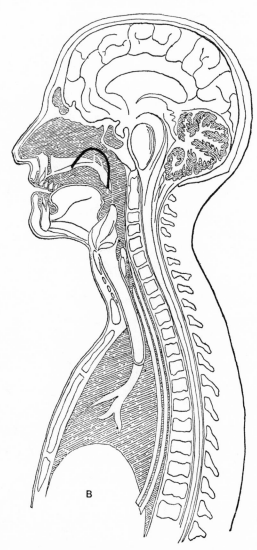

B

line denotes sensation of the form in slow progression of tones

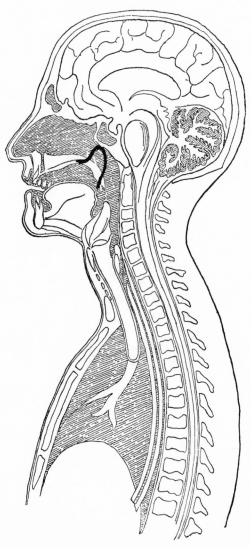

line denotes sensation for the propagation form

the larynx then is in a very low position, and thus is out of its way.

Furthermore, there is the unconstrained position of the larynx, which must be maintained without pressure of the throat muscles. From it the breath must stream forth evenly and uninterruptedly, to fill the form prepared for it by the tongue and palate and supported by the throat muscles.

This support must not, however, depend in the least upon *pressure*, — for the vibrating breath must float above, — but upon the greatest elasticity. One must play with the muscles, and be able to contract and relax them at pleasure, having thus perfect mastery over them. For this incessant practice is required, increasing control of the breath through the sense of hearing and the breath pressure.

At first a very strong will power is needed to hold the muscles tense without pressure; that is, to let the tone, as it were, soar through the throat, mouth, or cavities of the head.

The stronger the improper pressure in the production of the tone, the more difficult it is to get rid of. The result is simply, in other words, a strain. The contraction of the muscles must go only so far that they can be slowly relaxed; that is, can return to their normal position *easily*. Never must the neck be swelled up, or the veins in it stand out. Every convulsive or painful feeling is wrong.

SECTION VI

THE ATTACK

To attack a tone, the breath must be directed to a focal point on the palate, which lies under the critical point for each different tone; this must be done with a certain decisiveness. There must, however, be no pressure on this place; for the overtones must be able to soar above, and sound with, the tone. The palate has to furnish, besides, the top cover against which the breath strikes, also an extremely elastic floor for the breath sounding above it against the hard palate or in the nose.

This breath, by forming the overtones, makes certain the connection with the resonance of the head cavities.

In order to bring out the color of the tone the whirling currents must vivify all

the vowel sounds that enter into it, and draw
them into their circles with an ever-increas-
ing, soaring tide of sound.

The duration of the tone must be assured
by the gentle but uninterrupted outpouring
of the breath behind it.   Its strength must
be gained by the breath pressure and the
focal point on the palate, by the complete
utilization of the palatal resonance; without,
however, injuring the resonance of the head
cavities. (See plate, representing the attack.)

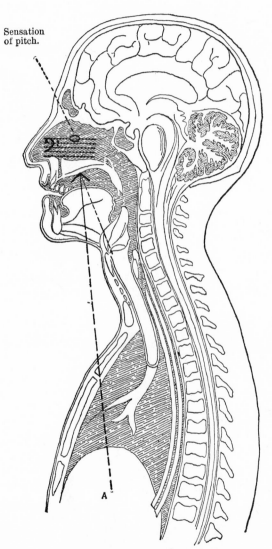

Sensation
of pitch.

A

line denotes sensation in the attack

SECTION VII

NASAL. NASAL SINGING

By raising the back of the tongue toward the soft palate and lowering the soft palate toward the tongue, we produce nasal sound, such as is heard in the pronunciation of the word "hanger," for instance. The air is then expelled chiefly through the nose. The nasal sound can be much exaggerated — something that very rarely happens; it can be much neglected — something that very often happens. Certain it is that it is not nearly enough availed of. That is my own every-day experience.

We Germans have only small opportunity to make the acquaintance of the nasal sound; we know it in only a few words: "Engel," "lange," "mangel," etc., — always where *ng* occurs before or after a vowel.

73

The French, on the contrary, always sing
and speak nasally, with the pillar of the
fauces raised high, and not seldom exaggerate
it. On account of the rounding up of the
whole soft palate, which, through the power
of habit, is cultivated especially by the
French to an extraordinary degree, and which
affords the breath an enormous space as a
resonating surface to act upon, their voices
often sound tremendous. The tenor Silva
is a good example of this. Such voices have
only the one drawback of easily becoming
monotonous. At first the power of the organ
astonishes us; the next time we are disap-
pointed — the tone color remains always the
same. The tone often even degenerates into
a hollow quality.

On the other hand, voices that are not
sufficiently nasal sound clear and expression-
less. Madame Melba, for instance, whose
voice is cultivated to favor the head tones, and
sounds equally well in all its ranges, apparently lowers the pillars of the fauces too

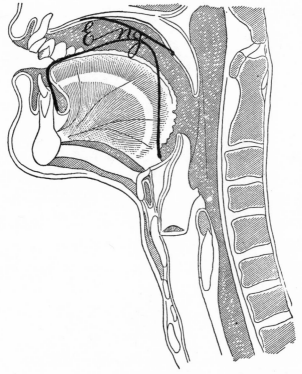

lines denote movement of the tongue and palate for the
nasal tone

much, and has her chief resonance in the
head cavities; she cannot draw upon the
palatal resonance for single accents of expression.   Consequently she loses in vocal
color.   This procedure, as soon as it becomes
a habit, results in monotony.

In the first case somewhat less, in the
second somewhat more, nasal resonance would
help to a greater variety of effect.

There are singers, too, who pursue the
middle path with consummate art.   Thus
Madame Sembrich, in recent years, appears
to have devoted very special study to nasal
tones, whereby her voice, especially in the
middle register, has gained greatly in warmth.

To fix the pupil's attention on the nasal
tone and the elasticity of the palate, he
should often be given exercises with French
words.

SECTION VIII

SINGING TOWARD THE NOSE. HEAD VOICE

WHEN the peak of the softest part of the palate is placed forward toward the nose, instead of being drawn up high behind the nose, as in the head voice (see plate, head voice and nasal tone), it forms a kind of nasal production which, as I have already said, cannot be studied enough, because it produces very noble tonal effects and extraordinary connections. It ought always to be employed. By it is effected the connection of tones with each other, from the front teeth back to a point under the nose; from the lower middle tones to the head tones. In truth, all the benefit of tonal connection depends upon this portion of the soft palate; that is, upon its conscious employment.

This is all that singers mean when they

speak of "nasal singing" — really only singing toward the nose.   The soft palate placed
toward the nose offers a resonating surface
for the tone.

The reason why teachers tell their pupils
so little of this is that many singers are
quite ignorant of what nasal singing means,
and are tormented by the idea of "singing
toward the nose," when by chance they hear
something about it.   They generally regard
the voice as one complete organ acting by
itself, which is once for all what it is.
What can be made of it through knowledge
of the functions of all the coöperating organs
they know nothing of.

Blind voices are often caused by the exaggerated practice of closing off the throat too
tightly from the head cavities; that is,
drawing the pillars of the fauces too far
toward the wall of the throat.   The large
resonating chamber thus formed yields tones
that are powerful close at hand, but they do
not carry, because they are poor in overtones.

The mistake consists in the practice of stretching the pillars too widely in the higher vocal ranges, also. In proportion as the pillars are extended, the breath spreads over the entire palate, instead of being concentrated on only one point of it, and bringing at the same time the resonance of the head cavities into play. The soft palate must first be drawn up to, then behind, the nose, and the attack of the higher tones be transferred thither. The pillars of the fauces must necessarily be relaxed by this action of the soft palate. Thereby breath is introduced into the cavities of the head to form the overtones, which contribute brilliancy and freshness to the voice.

Many singers persist in the bad habit here described, as long as nature can endure it; in the course of time, however, even with the most powerful physiques, they will begin to sing noticeably flat; with less powerful, the fatal tremolo will make its appearance, which results in the ruin of so many singers.

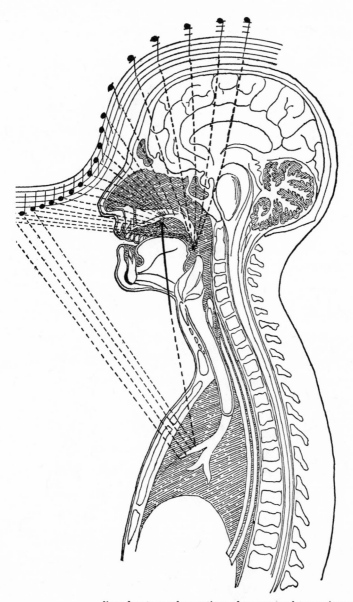

lines denote vocal sensations of soprano and tenor singers

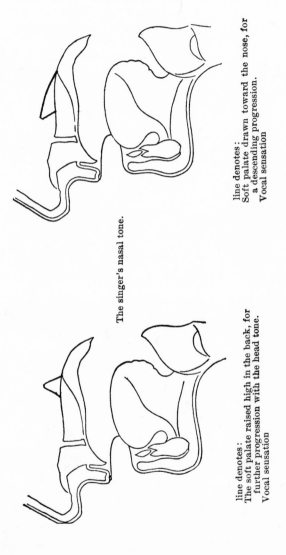

The singer's nasal tone.

line denotes:
Soft palate drawn toward the nose, for a descending progression.
Vocal sensation

line denotes:
The soft palate raised high in the back, for further progression with the head tone.
Vocal sensation

How often have I heard young singers say, " I no longer have the power to respond to the demands made upon me," whereas the trouble lies only in the insufficient use of the resonance of the head cavities. It should never be forgotten that as the posture of the voice changes, the position of the organs cannot remain the same.

SECTION IX

THE HEAD VOICE

THE head tone signifies, for all voices, from the deepest bass to the highest soprano, — excepting for the fact that it furnishes the overtones for each single tone of the whole vocal gamut, — youth. A voice without vibrancy is an *old* voice. The magic of youth, freshness, is given by the overtones that sound with every tone.

So to utilize the head voice (resonance of the head cavities) that every tone shall be able to "carry" and shall remain high enough to reach higher tones easily, is a difficult art, without which, however, the singer cannot reckon upon the durability of his voice. Often employed unconsciously, it is lost through heedlessness, mistaken method, or ignorance; and it can hardly

ever be regained, or, if at all, only through
the greatest sacrifice of time, trouble, and
patience.

The *pure* head voice (the third register)
is, on account of the thinness that it has by
nature, the neglected step-child of almost all
singers, male and female; its step-parents,
in the worst significance of the word, are
most singing teachers, male and female. It
is produced by the complete lowering of the
pillars of the fauces, while the softest point
of the palate — behind the nose — is thrown
up very high, seemingly, almost into the
head; in the highest position, as it were,
above the head.

The rear of the tongue stands high, but
is formed into a furrow, in order that the
mass of the tongue may not be in the way,
either in the throat or in the mouth. In
the very highest falsetto and head tones the
furrow is pretty well filled out, and then
no more breath at all reaches the palatal
resonance.

The larynx stands high — mine leans over to one side. (See plates of larynx.)

The vocal cords, which we cannot feel, now approach very near each other. The pupil should not read about them until he has learned to hear correctly. I do not intend to write a physiological work, but simply to attempt to examine certain infallible vocal sensations of the singer; point out ways to cure evils, and show how to gain a correct understanding of that which we lack.

Up to a certain pitch, with tenors as well as with sopranos, the head tones should be mixed with palatal resonance. With tenors this will be a matter of course, though with them the chest tones are much abused; with sopranos, however, a judicious mixture may be recommended because more expression is required (since the influence of Wagner has become paramount in interpreting the meaning of a composition, especially of the words) than in the brilliant fireworks of former

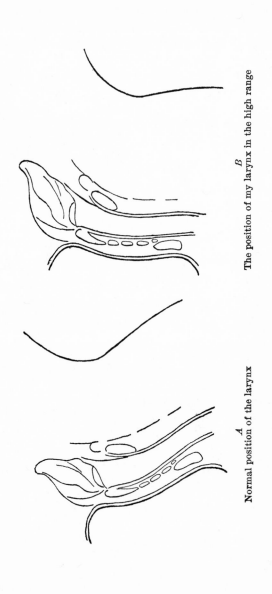

A

Normal position of the larynx

B

The position of my larynx in the high range

times. The head voice, too, must not be
regarded as a definite register of its own,
which is generally produced in the middle
range through too long a persistence in the
use of the palatal and nasal resonance. If
it is suddenly heard alone, after forcing tones
that have preceded it, which is not possible
under other circumstances, it is of course
noticeably thin, and stands out to its disadvantage — like every other sharply defined
register — from the middle tones. In the
formation of the voice no " register " should
exist or be created ; the voice must be made
even throughout its entire range. I do not
mean by this that I should sing neither with
chest tones nor with head tones. On the
contrary, the practised artist should have at
his command all manner of different means
of expression, that he may be able to use his
single tones, according to the expression
required, with widely diverse qualities of
resonance. This, too, must be cared for in
his studies. But these studies, because they

must fit each individual case, according to the genius or talent of the individual, can be imparted and directed only by a good teacher.

The head voice, when its value is properly appreciated, is the most valuable possession of all singers, male and female. It should not be treated as a Cinderella, or as a last resort, — as is often done too late, and so without results, because too much time is needed to regain it, when once lost, — but should be cherished and cultivated as a guardian angel and guide, like no other. Without its aid all voices lack brilliancy and carrying power; they are like a head without a brain. Only by constantly summoning it to the aid of all other registers is the singer able to keep his voice fresh and youthful. Only by a careful application of it do we gain that power of endurance which enables us to meet the most fatiguing demands. By it alone can we effect a complete equalization of the whole compass of all voices, and extend that compass.

This is the great secret of those singers who keep their voices young till they reach an advanced age. Without it all voices of which great exertions are demanded infallibly meet disaster. Therefore, the motto must be always, practice, and again, practice, to keep one's powers uninjured; practice brings freshness to the voice, strengthens the muscles, and is, for the singer, far more interesting than any musical composition.

If in my explanations I frequently repeat myself, it is done not unintentionally, but deliberately, because of the difficulty of the subject, as well as of the superficiality and negligence of so many singers who, after once hastily glancing through such a treatise, — if they consider it worth their while at all to inform themselves on the subject, — think they have done enough with it.

One must read continually, study constantly by one's self, to gain even a faint idea of the difficulty of the art of singing, of managing the voice, and even of one's own organs and mistakes, which are one's second self. The phenomenon of the voice is an elaborate complication of manifold functions which are united in an extremely limited space, to produce a single tone; functions which can only be heard, scarcely felt — indeed, should be felt as little as possible. Thus, in spite of ourselves, we can only come back again to the point from which we started, as in an eddy, repeating the explanations of the single functions, and relating them to each other.

Since in singing we sense none of the various activities of the cartilage, muscles, ligaments, and tendons that belong to the vocal apparatus, feel them only in their co-operation, and can judge of the correctness of their workings only through the ear, it would be absurd to think of them while singing. We are compelled, in spite of scientific knowledge, to direct our attention while practising, to the sensations of the voice, which are the only ones we can become

aware of, — sensations which are confined to
the very palpable functions of the organs of
breathing, the position of the larynx, of the
tongue, and of the palate, and finally, to the
sensation of the resonance of the head cavities. The perfect tone results from the combined operations of all these functions, the
sensations of which I undertake to explain,
and the control of which the ear alone can
undertake.

This is the reason why it is so important
to learn to hear one's self, and to sing in
such a way that one can always so hear.

Even in the greatest stress of emotion the
power of self-control must never be lost; you
must never allow yourself to sing in a
slovenly, that is, in a heedless, way, or to
exceed your powers, or even to reach their
extreme limit. That would be synonymous
with roughness, which should be excluded
from every art, especially in the art of song.
The listener must gain a pleasing impression from every tone, every expression of

the singer; much more may be given if desired.

Strength must not be confounded with
roughness; and the two must not go hand
in hand together. Phenomenal beings may
perhaps be permitted to go beyond the
strength of others; but to the others this
must remain forbidden. It cannot become
a regular practice, and is best limited to
the single phenomenon. We should otherwise soon reach the point of crudest realism,
from which at best we are not far removed.
Roughness will never attain artistic justifica-
tion, not even in the case of the greatest
individual singers, because it is an offence.

The public should witness from interpreta-
tive art only what is good and noble on
which to form its taste; there should be
nothing crude or commonplace put before
it, which it might consider itself justified
in taking as an example.

Of the breath sensation I have already
spoken at length. I must add that it is

often very desirable in singing to breathe
through the nose with the mouth closed;
although when this is done, the raising of
the palate becomes less certain, as it happens
somewhat later than when the breath is
taken with the mouth open. It has, however, this disadvantage, that neither cold air
nor dust is drawn into the larynx and air
passages. I take pleasure in doing it very
often. At all events, the singer should often
avail himself of it.

We feel the larynx when the epiglottis
springs up ("stroke of the glottis," if the
tone is taken from below upward). We can
judge whether the epiglottis springs up quickly
enough if the breath comes out in a full
enough stream to give the tone the necessary resonance. The low position of the
larynx can easily be secured by pronouncing
the vowel *oo;* the high, by pronouncing the
vowel *ā*. Often merely thinking of one or
the other is enough to put the larynx, tongue,
and palate in the right relations to each

other.   Whenever I sing in a high vocal range, I can plainly feel the larynx rise and take a diagonal position.   (See plate.)

The movement is, of course, very slight. Yet I have the feeling in my throat as if everything in it was stretching.   I feel the pliability of my organs plainly as soon as I sing higher.

SECTION X

SENSATION AND POSITION OF THE TONGUE

WE feel the placing of its tip against or beneath the front teeth; and place the tip very low, so that it really curves over in front. (See plate.)

Its hinder part must be drawn back toward the palate, in the pronunciation of every letter.

Furthermore, by looking in the mirror we can *see* that the sides of the tongue are raised as soon as we wish to form a furrow in it; that is, as we *must* do to produce the palatal resonance. (Only in the head tone — that is, the use of the resonance of the head cavities without the added palatal resonance — has the tongue no furrow; it must, however, lie very high, since otherwise its mass, when it lies flat, presses against the larynx and produces pinched or otherwise disagreeable tones.)

The best way is to get the mass of the tongue out of the way by forming the furrow in it. In high notes, when the larynx must stand as high as possible, the back of the tongue also must stand very high; but since there is a limit to this, we are often compelled to make the larynx take a lower position.

Correct.   Incorrect.

The correct position of the tongue, preparatory to singing, is gained by saying the vowel sound *aou*, as if about to yawn.

The tongue must not scrape around upward with its tip. As soon as the tip has been employed in the pronunciation of the consonants *l*, *n*, *s*, *t*, and *z*, in which its service is very short and sharp, it must return to its former position, and keep to it.

It is best to watch the movements of the tongue in the mirror until we have formed the correct habit permanently. The more elastic the tongue is in preparing the form for the breath to pass through, the stiller will it appear, the stiller will it feel to us. It is well, however, for a considerable time to watch in a mirror all functions of the organs that can be seen; the expression of the face, the position of the mouth, and the movement of the lips.

SECTION XI

THE SENSATIONS OF THE PALATE

THE sensations of the palate are best made
clear to us by raising the softest part behind
the nose. This part is situated very far back.
Try touching it carefully with the finger.
This little part is of immeasurable importance
to the singer. By raising it the entire
resonance of the head cavities is brought into
play — consequently the head tones are produced. When it is raised, the pillars of the
fauces are lowered. In its normal position
it allows the pillars to be distended and to
close the head cavities off from the throat, in
order to produce the chest tones; that is, to
permit the breath to make fullest use of the
palatal resonance. As soon as the soft palate is lowered under the nose, it makes a
point of resonance for the middle range of

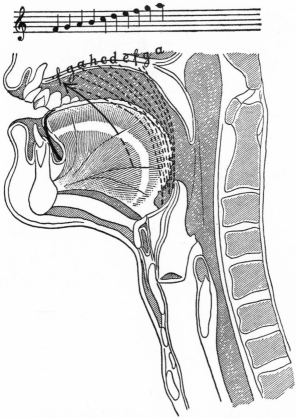

lines denote middle range of soprano, contralto, and tenor.
In the German names of the notes, *h* represents *b* in the English

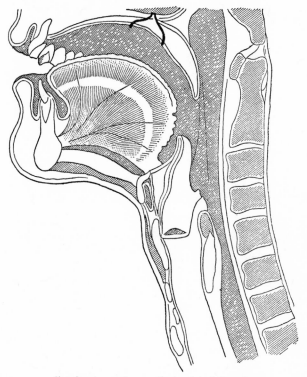

line denotes peak, or softest point of the palate.

voice, by permitting the overtones to resound at the same time in the nose. (See plate, middle range.)

Thus the palate performs the whole work so far as concerns the different resonances, which can be united and separated by it, but must *always work together in close relation, always bound together in all tones, in all kinds of voices.*

The lowest chest tones of the bass, the highest head tones of the soprano, are thus the two poles between which the entire gamut of all voices can be formed. From this it can be perceived that with a certain degree of skill and willingness to work, every voice will be capable of great extension.

SECTION XII

THE SENSATION OF THE RESONANCE OF THE HEAD CAVITIES

THE sensation of the resonance of the head cavities is perceived chiefly by those who are unaccustomed to using the head tones. The resonance against the occipital walls of the head cavities when the head tones are employed, at first causes a very marked irritation of the nerves of the head and ear. But this disappears as soon as the singer gets accustomed to it. The head tones can be used and directed by the breath only with a clear head. The least depression such as comes with headaches, megrim, or moodiness may have the worst effect, or even make their use quite impossible. This feeling of oppression is lost after regular, conscious practice, by which all unnecessary and disturbing pressure is avoided. In singing very high head tones I have a feeling as if they lay high above the head, as if I were setting them off into the air. (See plate.)

Here, too, is the explanation of singing *in the neck.* The breath, in all high tones which are much mixed with head tones or use them entirely, passes very far back, directly from the throat into the cavities of the head, and thereby, and through the oblique position of the larynx, gives rise to the sensations just described. A singer who inhales and exhales carefully, that is, with knowledge of the physiological processes, will always have a certain feeling of pleasure, an attenuation in the throat as if it were stretching itself upward. The bulging out of veins in the neck, that can so often be seen in singers, is as wrong as the swelling up of the neck, looks very ugly, and is not without danger from congestion.

With rapid scales and trills one has the feeling of great firmness of the throat muscles, as well as of a certain stiffness of the larynx. (See "Trills.") An unsteady movement of the latter, this way and that, would be disadvantageous to the trill, to rapid scales, as well as to the cantilena. For this reason, because the changing movements of the organs must go on quite imperceptibly and inaudibly, it must be more like a shifting than a movement. In rapid scales the lowest tone must be "placed" with a view to the production of the highest, and in descending, the greatest care must be exercised that the tone shall not tumble over each other single, but shall produce the sensation of closely connected sounds, through being bound to the high tone position and pressed toward the nose.

In this all the participating vocal organs must be able to keep up a muscular contraction, often very rigid: a thing that is to be achieved only gradually through long years of careful and regular study. Excessive practice is of no use in this — only regular

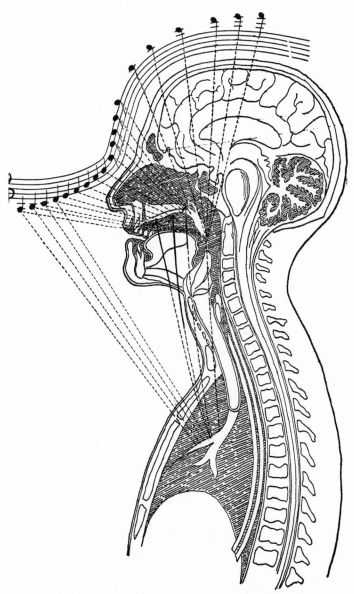

line denotes vocal sensation of soprano and tenor

and intelligent practice; and success comes only in course of time.

Never should the muscular contractions become convulsive and produce pressure which the muscles cannot endure for a long time. They must respond to all necessary demands upon their strength, yet remain elastic in order that, easily relaxing or again contracting, they may promptly adapt themselves to every nuance in tone and accent desired by the singer.

A singer can become and continue to be master of his voice and means of expression only as long as he practises daily correct vocal gymnastics. In this way alone can he obtain unconditional mastery over his muscles, and, through them, of the finest controlling apparatus, of the beauty of his voice, as well as of the art of song as a whole.

Training the muscles of the vocal organs so that their power to contract and relax to all desired degrees of strength, throughout the entire gamut of the voice, is always at command, makes the master singer.

As I have already said, the idea of "singing forward" leads very many singers to force the breath from the mouth without permitting it to make full use of the resonating surfaces that it needs, yet it streams forth from the larynx really very far back in the throat, and the straighter it rises in a column behind the tongue, the better it is for the tone. The tongue must furnish the surrounding form for this, for which reason it must not lie flat in the mouth. (See plate, the tongue.)

The whirling currents of tone circling around their focal point (the attack) find a cup-shaped resonating cavity when they reach the front of the mouth and the lips, which, through their extremely potent auxiliary movements, infuse life and color into the tone and the word. Of equal importance are the unimpeded activity of the whirling currents of sound and their complete filling of the

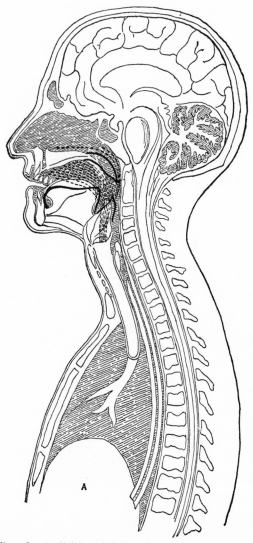

A

lines denote division of the breath in the palatal resonance:
lower range of male and female voices

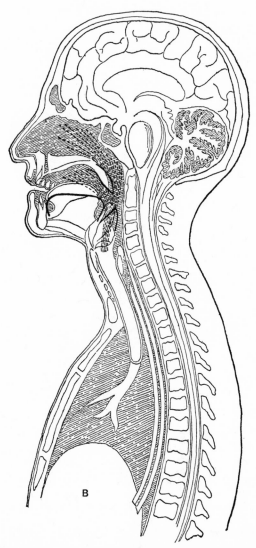

B

lines denote division of the breath in the middle range and
higher middle range

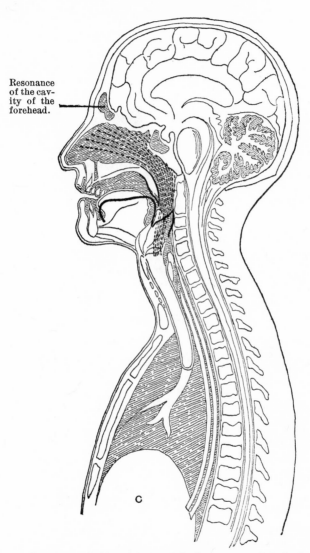

Resonance
of the cav-
ity of the
forehead.

C

lines denote division of the breath in the resonance of the head
cavities, high range

resonating spaces in the back of the throat, the pillars of the fauces, and the head cavities in which the vocalized breath must be kept soaring above the larynx and *soaring undisturbed.*

In the lowest range of the voice the entire palate from the front teeth to the rear wall of the throat must be thus filled. (See plate.)

With higher tones the palate is lowered, the nostrils are inflated, and above the hard palate a passage is formed for the overtones. (See plate.)

This air which soars above must, however, not be in the least compressed; the higher the tone, the less pressure should there be; for here, too, whirling currents are formed, which must be neither interrupted nor destroyed. The breath must be carried along on the wall of the throat without compression, in order to accomplish its work. (See plate, high tones.)

Singing forward, then, does not mean pressing the whole of the *breath* or the tone forward, but only part of it; that is, in the middle register, finding a resonating focus in front, caused by the lowering of the front of the palate. This permits a free course only to that part of the breath which is used up by the whirling currents in the resonant throat form, and serves to propagate the outer waves, and carry them farther through space.

SECTION XIII

SINGING COVERED

WE sing covered as soon as the soft palate is lowered toward the nose (that is, in the middle register), and the resonance and attack are transferred thither so that the breath can flow over the soft palate through the nose.

This special function of the palate, too, should be carefully prepared for in the tones that precede it, and mingled with them, in order not to be heard so markedly as it often is. In men's voices this is much more plainly audible than in women's; but both turn it to account equally on different tones. This often produces a new register that should not be produced. This belongs to the chapter on registers.

The tone is concentrated on the front of the palate instead of being spread over all of it — but this must not be done too suddenly. [See illustrations on pages 127, 129, 131, 133.]

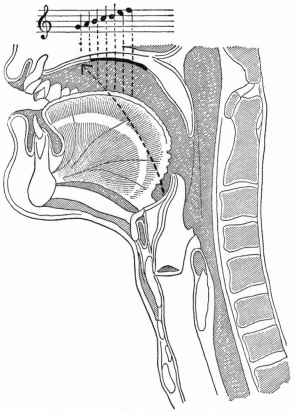

lines denote covered tones for contralto and soprano

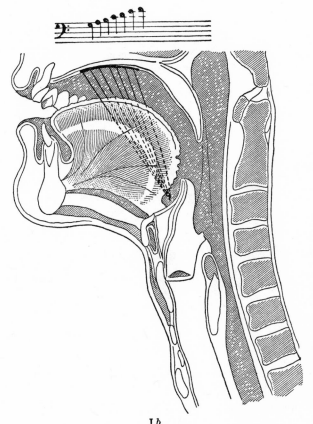

I b

lines denote covered tones for bass and baritone

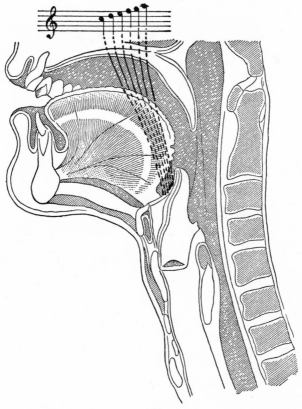

II *b*

lines denote change of attack.   (Soprano, contralto, and tenor.)

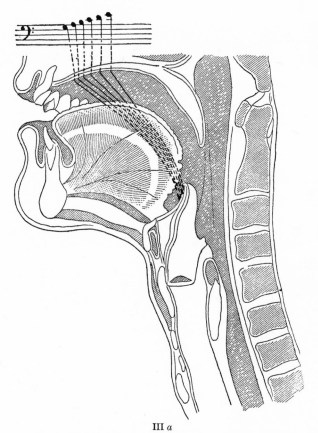

III *a*

lines denote change of attack.   (Bass and baritone.)

SECTION XIV

ON VOCAL REGISTERS

WHAT is a vocal register?

A series of tones sung in a certain way, which are produced by a certain position of the vocal organs — larynx, tongue, and palate. Every voice includes three registers — chest, middle, and head. But all are not employed in every class of voice.

Two of them are often found connected to a certain extent in beginners; the third is usually much weaker, or does not exist at all. Only very rarely is a voice found naturally equalized over its whole compass.

Do registers exist by nature? No. It may be said that they are created through long years of speaking in the vocal range that is easiest to the person, or in one adopted by imitation, which then becomes a fixed habit. If this is coupled with a natural and proper working of the muscles of the vocal organs, it may become the accustomed range, strong in comparison with others, and form a register by itself. This fact would naturally be appreciated only by singers.

If, on the other hand, the muscles are wrongly employed in speaking, not only the range of voice generally used, but the whole voice as well, may be made to sound badly. So, in every voice, one or another range may be stronger or weaker; and this is, in fact, almost always the case, since mankind speaks and sings in the pitch easiest or most accustomed, without giving thought to the proper position of the organs in relation to each other; and people are rarely made to pay attention as children to speaking clearly and in an agreeable voice. In the most fortunate instances the range thus practised reaches limits on both sides, not so much those of the person's power, as those set

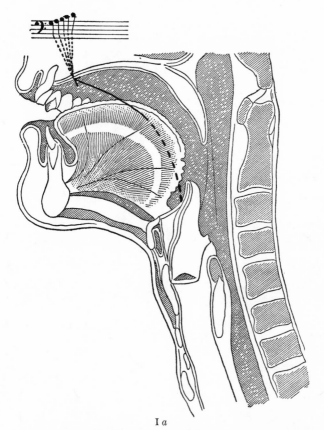

I a

lines denote a register is formed when as many tones as possible are forced upon one and the same point of resonance
(Bass and baritone.)

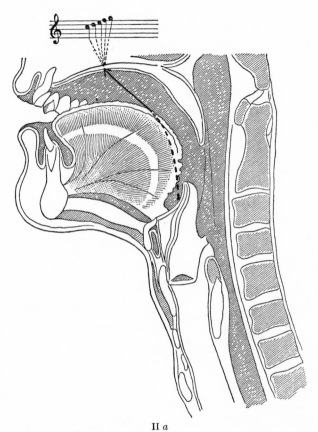

II _a_

lines denote a register is formed when as many tones as possible are forced upon one and the same point of resonance.
(Soprano, contralto, and tenor.)

by his lack of skill, or practice. Limitations
are put on the voice through taking account
only of the easiest and most accustomed
thing, without inquiring into the potentiali-
ties of the organs or the demands of art.

Now, suppose such a peculiarity which includes, let us say, three or four tones, is
extended to six or eight, then, in the course
of time, in the worst cases, a break is produced at the outside limits. In the most
favorable cases the tones lying next beyond
these limits are conspicuously weak and without power compared with those previously
forced. This one way of singing can be used
no farther; another must be taken up, only,
perhaps, to repeat farther the incorrect procedure.

Three such limits or ways of singing can
be found and used. Chest, middle, and head
voice, all three form registers when exaggerated; but they should be shaded off and
melt into each other. The organs, through
the skilful training of the teacher, as well

as by the exercise of the pupil's talent and
industry, must be accustomed to taking such
positions that one register leads into another
imperceptibly. In this way beauty, equality,
and increased compass of the voice will be
made to enhance its usefulness.

When the three ways of singing are too
widely different and too sharply contrasted,
they become separate registers. These are
everywhere accepted as a matter of course,
and for years have been a terror in the
teaching of singing, that has done more than
anything else to create a dreadful bewilder-
ment among singers and teachers. To eradi-
cate it is probably hopeless. Yet, these registers are nothing more than three disconnected
manners of using the vocal and resonating
apparatus.

With all the bad habits of singers, with
all the complete ignorance of cause and
effect, that prevail, it is not surprising that
some pretend to tell us that there are two,
three, four, or five registers, although as a

matter of fact there can be at most three in any voice. It will be much more correct to call every tone of every voice by the name of a new additional register, for in the end, every tone will and *must* be taken in a different relation, with a different position of the organs, although the difference may be imperceptible, if it is to have its proper place in the whole. People cling to the appellations of chest, middle, and head *register*, confounding voice with register, and making a hopeless confusion, from which only united and very powerful forces can succeed in extricating them.

As long as the word "register" is kept in use, the registers will not disappear. And yet, the register question must be swept away, to give place to another class of ideas, sounder views on the part of teachers, and a truer conception on the part of singers and pupils.

SECTION XV

DEVELOPMENT AND EQUALIZATION

NATURALLY, a singer can devote more strength to the development of one or two connected ranges of his voice than to a voice perfectly equalized in all its accessible ranges. For this are required many years of the most patient study and observation, often a long-continued or entire sacrifice of one or the other limit of a range for the benefit of the next-lying weaker one; of the head voice especially, which, if unmixed, sounds uneven and thin in comparison with the middle range, until by means of practised elasticity of the organs and endurance of the throat muscles a positive equalization can take place.

Voices which contain only one or two registers are called short voices, for their availability is as limited as they are themselves.

Yet it must be remembered that all voices alike, whether short or long, even those of the most skilful singers, when age comes on, are apt to lose their highest ranges, if they are not continually practised throughout their entire compass with the subtlest use of the head tones. Thence it is to be concluded that a singer ought always to extend the compass of his voice as far as possible, in order to be certain of possessing the compass that he needs.

On the formation of the organs depends much of the character of the voice. There are strong, weak, deep, and high voices by nature; but every voice, by means of proper study, can attain a certain degree of strength, flexibility, and compass.

Unfortunately, stubbornness enters largely into this question, and often works in opposition to the teacher. Many, for instance, wish to be altos, either because they are

afraid of ruining their voices by working for
a higher compass, or because it is easier for
them, even if their voices are not altos at
all.

Nowadays operas are no longer composed
for particular singers and the special characteristics of their voices.   Composers and
librettists express what they feel without
regard to an alto singer who has no high
C or a soprano who has no low A flat or
G.   But the *artist* will always find what
he needs.

Registers exist in the voices of almost all
singers, but they ought not to be heard,
ought not, indeed, to exist.   Everything
should be sung with a mixed voice in such
a way that no tone is forced at the expense
of any other.   To avoid monotony the singer
should have at his disposal a wealth of means
of expression in all ranges of his voice.   (See
the Varieties of Attack and Dynamic Power.)
Before all else he should have knowledge of
the advantages in the resonance of certain

tones, and of their connection with each other. The *soul* must provide the color; skill and knowledge as to cause and effect, management of the breath, and perfection of the throat formation must give the power to produce every dynamic gradation and detail of expression. Registers are, accordingly, produced when the singer forces a series of tones, generally ascending, upon one and the same resonating point, instead of remembering that in a progression of tones no one tone can be exactly like another, because the position of the organs must be different for each. The palate must remain elastic from the front teeth to its hindmost part, mobile and susceptible, though imperceptibly, to all changes. Very much depends on the continuous harmony of action of the soft and hard palate, which must always be in full evidence, the raising and extension of the former producing changes in the tone. If, as often happens when the registers are sharply defined, tones fall into a *cul de sac*,

escape into another register is impossible,
without a jump, which may lead to disaster.
With every tone that the singer has to sing,
he must always have the feeling that he
can go higher, and that the attack for different tones must not be forced upon one
and the same point.

The larynx must not be *suddenly* pressed
down nor jerked up, except when this is desired as a special effect.   That is, when one
wishes to make a transition, *legato*, from a
chest tone to a tone in the middle or head
register, as the old Italians used to do, and
as I, too, learned to do, thus : —

In this case the chest tone is attacked
very nasal, in order that the connection may
remain to the upper note, and the larynx
is suddenly jerked up to the high tone.
This was called breaking the tone ; it was
very much used, and gave fine effects when

it was well done. I use it to-day, especially in Italian music, where it belongs. It is an exception to the rule for imperceptible or inaudible change of position of the organs, — that it should not be made *suddenly*.

The scale proceeds from one semitone to another; each is different; each, as you go on, requires greater height, wherefore the position of the organs cannot remain the same for several different tones. But, as there should never be an abrupt change audible in the way of singing, so should there never be an abrupt change felt in the sensations of the singer's throat. Every tone must be imperceptibly prepared in an elastic channel and must produce an easy feeling in the singer, as well as an agreeable impression upon the listener.

The small peak indicated in the illustration is enormously extensible and can be shifted into infinite varieties of position. However unimportant its raising and lowering may appear, they are nevertheless of

great importance for the tone and the singer.
The focal point of the breath, that forms
simultaneously the attack and the body of
the tone, by the operation of the abdominal
breath pressure against the chest, is always
firmly placed on, beneath, or behind the nose.
Without body even the finest pianissimo has
no significance.   The very highest unmixed
head tones are an exception, and they can
express nothing.   There can be no body expected in them.   Their soaring quality of
sound endures no pressure, and consequently
gives no expression, which is possible only
through an admixture of palatal resonance.
Their only significance is gained through
their pure euphony.

All vowels, too, must keep their point of
resonance uninterruptedly on the palate.
All beauty in the art of song, in cantilena
as well as in all technique, consists chiefly
in uninterrupted connection between the
tone and the word, in the flexible connection of the soft palate with the hard, in the

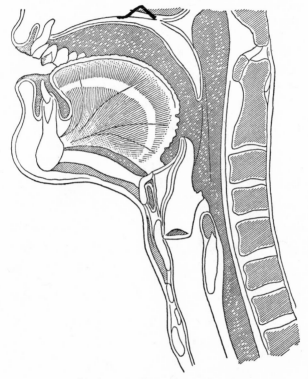

line denotes softest point on the palate

continually elastic adjustment of the former
to the latter.   This means simply the elastic
form, which the breath must fill in every
corner of resonating surface without interruption, as long as the tone lasts.

If the singer will control his tone, — and
in practising he must always do so, — he
needs only to test it to see whether he can
easily make it softer without perceptible
change in the position of the organs, and
carry it higher toward the nose and the
cavities of the forehead; that is, prepare a
form for its continuation upward.

*In this way he can learn how much height
a tone needs without being too high, and how
much it often lacks in height and duration
to sound high enough.*

In this way remarkable faults become evident!   The reason why a tone sounds too
low — the so-called transition tones from the
lower to the middle range and from this
to the higher, come up for consideration
chiefly — is that the pillars of the fauces

are raised too high toward the back, preventing the head tones from sounding at the same time; or the soft palate is lowered too far under the nose, which results in pressing the tone too long and too far toward the teeth. This fault is met with in very many singers, in all kinds of voices, and in almost the same places. It comes only from an unyielding retention of the same resonating point for several tones and a failure to bring in the resonance of the head cavities. The " propagation form," or continuing form,[1] must always be prepared consciously, for without it artistic singing is not to be thought of.

The neglect of this most important principle usually results in overstraining the vocal cords and throat muscles. This is followed first by singing flat, and later by the appearance of the hideous tremolo (see Tremolo) to

---

[1] " Fortpflanzungsform ": the preparation made in the vocal organs for taking the next tone before leaving the one under production, so that the succeeding tones shall all be of like character and quality.

which so many singers fall victims. The
cause of a tone's being too sharp is the dwell-
ing too long on the resonance of the head cavities, where the tone should already have been
mixed with palatal resonance. With very
young voices this can easily happen, and
can also result from weariness, when the
bodily strength is not developed sufficiently
to endure the fatigue of practising. A very
circumspect course must then be followed.

SECTION XVI

WHITE VOICES

THERE are also singers, male and female, who use too much head tone through their entire compass; such voices are called "white." Their use of the palatal resonance being insufficient, they are not able to make a deeper impression, because their power of expression is practically nothing. Frau Wedekind and Madame Melba are instances of this. In such cases it would be advisable to raise the pillars of the fauces a little higher, and place the larynx somewhat lower, and to mingle judiciously with all the other vowels, the vowel sound *oo*, that requires a lower position of the larynx. The voices would become warmer and would sound more expressive. As soon as the singer is able to create easily and inaudibly on every tone the correct propagation form for the next tone, all questions as to register must disappear. He must not, however, be drilled on *registers;* several tones must not be forced on one and the same point. Every tone should be put naturally into its own place; should receive the pitch, duration, and strength it needs for its perfection. And one master rules it all, — the ear!

The goal is, unfortunately, so seldom reached because it can be reached only through the moderation that comes from mastery; and, alas! only true masters practise it.

It may be accepted as true that the lower ranges of the voice have the greatest strength, the middle ranges the greatest power of expression, the higher the greatest carrying power.

The best mixture — all three together — may be developed to the highest art by the skill of the individual, often, indeed, only by a good ear for it. Whenever expression of the word's significance, beauty of

the vocal material, and perfection of phrasing
are found united in the highest degree, it is
due either to knowledge or to a natural skill
in the innumerable ways of fitting the sung
word to the particular resonance — connections that are suitable to realize its significance, and hence its spirit. They are brought
out by a stronger inclination toward one or the
other of the resonance surfaces, without, however, injuring the connection or the beauty
of the musical phrase. Here æsthetic feeling plays the chief part, for whatever may
be its power and its truthfulness, the result
must always be beautiful, — that is, restrained
within proper limits.

This law, too, remains the same for all
voices. It is a question of the entire compass
of a voice trained for artistic singing, one
that is intrusted with the greatest of tasks,
to interpret works of art that are no popular
songs, but, for the most part, human trage-
dies. Most male singers — tenors especially
— consider it beneath them, generally, indeed,

unnatural or ridiculous, to use the falsetto, which is a part of all male voices, as the head tones are a part of all female voices. They do not understand how to make use of its assistance, because they often have no idea of its existence, or know it only in its unmixed purity — that is, its thinnest quality. Of its proper application they have not the remotest conception. Their singing is generally in accordance with their ignorance.

The mixture is present by nature in all kinds of voices, but singers must possess the skill and knowledge to employ it, else the natural advantage goes for nothing.

SECTION XVII

THEODOR WACHTEL

THE most perfect singer that I remember
in my Berlin experience was Theodor Wachtel
in this respect, that with his voice of rare
splendor, he united all that vocal art which,
as it seems, is destined quite to disappear
from among us. How beautiful were his
coloratura, his trills, — simply flawless!
Phrasing, force, fulness of tone, and beauty
were perfect, musically without a blemish.
If he did not go outside the range of Arnold,
G. Brown, Stradella, Vasco, the Postillion
and Lionel, it was probably because he felt
that he was not equal to interpreting the
Wagnerian spirit. In this he was very wise.
As one of the first of vocal artists, whose
voice was superbly trained and was preserved
to the end of his life, I have had to pay

to Wachtel the tribute of the most complete admiration and recognition, in contrast to many others who thought themselves greater than he, and yet were not worthy to unloose the latchet of his shoes.

Recently the little Italian tenor Bonci has won my hearty admiration for his splendidly equalized voice, his perfect art, and his knowledge of his resources; and notwithstanding the almost ludicrous figure that he cut in serious parts, he elicited hearty applause. Cannot German tenors, too, learn to sing *well*, even if they do interpret Wagner? Will they not learn, for the sake of this very master, that it is their duty not to use their voices recklessly?

Is it not disrespectful toward our greatest masters that they always have to play hide and seek with the *bel canto*, the trill, and coloratura? Not till one has fully realized the difficulties of the art of song, does it really become of value and significance. Not till then are one's eyes opened to the duty owed not only to one's self but to the public.

The appreciation of a difficulty makes study doubly attractive ; the laborious ascent of a summit which no one can contest, is the attainment of a goal.

Voices in which the palatal resonance — and so, power — is the predominating factor, are the hardest to manage and to preserve. They are generally called chest voices. Uncommon power and fulness of tone in the middle ranges are extremely seductive. Only rarely are people found with sense enough to renounce such an excess of fulness in favor of the head tones, — that is, the least risky range to exploit and preserve, — even if this has to be done only temporarily.

Copious vocal resources may with impunity be brought before the public and thereby submitted to strain, only after long and regular study.

The pure head tone, without admixture

of palatal resonance, is feeble close at hand,
but penetrating and of a carrying power
equalled by no other. Palatal resonance
without admixture of the resonance of the
head cavities (head tones) makes the tone
very powerful when heard near by, but
without vibrancy for a large auditorium.
This is the proof of how greatly *every* tone
needs the proper admixture.

SECTION XVIII

THE HIGHEST HEAD TONES

As we have already seen, there is almost no limit to the height that can be reached by the pure head tone without admixture of palatal resonance. Very young voices, especially, can reach such heights, for without any strain they possess the necessary adaptability and skill in the adjustment to each other of the larynx, tongue, and pillars of the fauces. A skill that rests on ignorance of the true nature of the phenomenon must be called pure chance, and thus its disappearance is as puzzling to teacher and listener as its appearance had been in the first place. How often is it paired with a total lack of ability to produce anything but the highest head tones! As a general rule such voices have a very short lease of

162

life, because their possessors are exploited
as wonders, before they have any conception of the way to use them, of tone, right
singing, and of cause and effect in general.
An erroneous pressure of the muscles, a
wrong movement of the tongue (raising the
tip, for instance,　　　　), an attempt to increase the strength of the tone, — all these
things extinguish quickly and for all time the
wonder-singer's little light.

We Lehmann children in our youth could
sing to the very highest pitch. It was
nothing for my sister Marie to strike the
4-line *e* a hundred times in succession, and
trill on it for a long time. She could have
sung in public at the age of seven. But since
our voices, through the circumstances of our
life and surroundings, were forced to early
exertions, they lost their remarkable high
notes; yet enough was left to sing the *Queen
of Night* (in Mozart's opera " Die Zauber-
flöte"), with the high *f*.

After I had been compelled to use my lower

and middle ranges much more, in the study of dramatic parts, I omitted the highest notes from my practice, but could not then always have relied on them. Now that I know on what it all depends, it is very easy for me to strike high *f*, not only in passing, but to combine it with any tone through three octaves. But upon the least pressure by any organ, the head resonance loses its brilliancy; that is, the breath no longer streams into the places where it should, and can create no more whirling currents of sound to fill the spaces.

But one should not suppose that the head tones have no power. When they are properly used, their vibrancy is a substitute for any amount of power.

As soon as the head tones come into consideration, one should *never* attempt to sing an open *ah*, because on *ah* the tongue lies flattest. One should think of an *ā*, and in the highest range even an *ē*; should mix the *ā* and *ē* with the *ah*, and thereby produce a position of the tongue and soft palate that

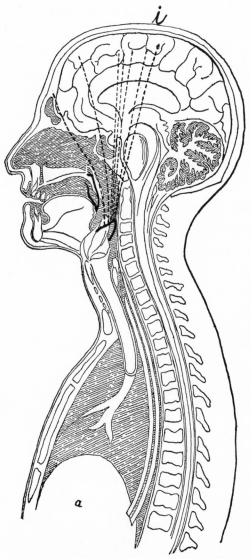

lines denote vocal sensation in the highest head tones
without mixture

makes the path clear for the introduction of
the breath into the cavities of the head.

Singers who, on the other hand, pronounce
ā and ē too sharply, need only introduce an
admixture of *oo*; they thereby lower the
position of the larynx, and thus give the
vowel and tone a darker color.

Since the stream of breath in the highest
tones produces currents whirling with great
rapidity, the more rapidly the higher the tone
is, the slightest pressure that may injure the
form in which they circulate may ruin
the evenness of the tone, its pitch, perhaps
the tone itself.   Each high tone must *soar
gently*, like the overtones.

The upper limits of a bass and baritone
voice are

where, consequently, the tones must be mixed.
Pure head tones, that is, falsetto, are never
demanded higher than this.   I regard it, how-

ever, as absolutely necessary for the artist to
give consideration to his falsetto, that he
may include it among his known resources.
Neither a bass nor a baritone should neglect
to give it the proper attention, and both
should learn to use it as one of their most
important auxiliary forces.

With what mastery did Betz make use of
it; how noble and beautiful his voice sounded
in all its ranges; of what even strength it
was, and how infallibly fresh! And let no
one believe that Nature gave it to him thus.
As a beginner in Berlin he was quite unsatis-
factory. He had the alternative given him
either to study with great industry or to seek
another engagement, for his successor had
already been selected. Betz chose to devote
himself zealously to study; he began also to
play the 'cello; he learned to *hear*, and finally
raised himself to be one of our first singers,
in many rôles never to be forgotten. Betz
knew, like myself, many things that to-day
are neither taught nor learned.

SECTION XIX

EXTENSION OF THE COMPASS AND EQUALIZATION OF REGISTERS

The whole secret of both consists in the proper raising and lowering of the soft palate, and the pillars of the fauces connected with it. This divides into two resonating divisions the breath coming from the source of supply, and forced against the chest, whereby it is put under control, as it escapes vocalized from the larynx. It consists also in the singer's natural adaptability and skill, in so placing the palate and resonance of the head cavities, or keeping them in readiness for every tone, as the pitch, strength, and duration of the individual tones or series of connected tones, with their propagation form, shall demand.

SECTION XX

THE TREMOLO

BIG voices, produced by large, strong organs, through which the breath can flow in a broad, powerful stream, are easily disposed to suffer from the tremolo, because the outflow of the breath against the vocal cords occurs too *immediately*. The breath is sent directly out from the lungs and the body, instead of being driven by the abdominal pressure forward against the chest and the controlling apparatus. Not till this has been done, should it be admitted, in the smallest amounts, and under control to the vocal cords. It does not pause, but streams through them without burdening them, though keeping them always more or less stretched, in which the muscular power of contraction and relaxation assists. Streaming *gently* out from the vocal cords, it is now led, with the support of the tongue, to its resonance chambers, all the corners of which it fills up equally. Even the strongest vocal cords cannot for any length of time stand the uncontrolled pressure of the breath. They lose their tension, and the result is the tremolo.

In inhaling, the chest should be raised not at all or but very little. (For this reason exercises for the expansion of the chest must be practised.) The pressure of the breath *against* the chest must be maintained as long as it is desired to sustain a tone or sing a phrase. As soon as the pressure of the abdomen and chest ceases, the tone and the breath are at an end. Not till toward the very end of the breath, that is, of the tone or the phrase, should the pressure be slowly relaxed, and the chest slowly sink.

While I am singing, I must press the breath against the chest *evenly*, for in this

way alone can it be directed evenly against
the vocal cords, which is the chief factor
in a steady tone and the only possible and
proper use of the vocal cords.

The uninterrupted control of the breath
pressure against the chest gives to the tone,
as soon as it has found a focal point on the
raised palate at the attack, the basis, the
body, which must be maintained even in
the softest pianissimo. Control of the breath
should never cease. The tone should never
be made too strong to be kept under control,
nor too weak to be kept under control.
This should be an inflexible rule for the
singer.

I direct my whole attention to the pressure
against the chest, which forms the door of
the supply chamber of breath. Thence I
admit to the vocal cords uninterruptedly only
just so much as I wish to admit. I must
not be stingy, nor yet extravagant with it.
Besides giving steadiness, the pressure against
the chest (the controlling apparatus) estab-

lishes the strength and the duration of the
tone. Upon the proper control depends the
length of the breath, which, without interruption, rises from here toward the resonating chambers, and, expelled into the elastic

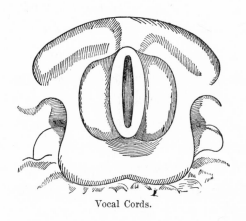

Vocal Cords.

form of the resonating apparatus, there must
obey our will.

It can now be seen how easily the vocal
cords can be injured by an uncontrolled
current of breath, if it is directed against
them in all its force. One need only see a
picture of the vocal cords to understand the
folly of exposing these delicate little bands

to the explosive force of the breath. They
cannot be protected too much; and also, they
cannot be too carefully exercised. They
must be spared all work not properly theirs;
this must be put upon the chest tension
muscles, which in time learn to endure an
out-and-out thump.

Even the vibrato, to which full voices are
prone, should be nipped in the bud, for
gradually the tremolo, and later even worse,
is developed from it. Life can be infused into
the tone by means of the lips — that is, in a
way that will do no harm. But of that later.

Vibrato is the first stage, tremolo the
second; a third and last, and much more
hopeless, shows itself in flat singing on the
upper middle tones of the register. Refer-
able in the same way to the overburdening
of the vocal cords is the excessive straining
of the throat muscles, which, through continual constriction, lose their power of *elastic*
contraction and relaxation because pitch and
duration of the tone are gained in an in-

correct way, by forcing. Neither should be forced; pitch should be merely maintained, as it were, soaring; strength should not be gained by a cramped compression of the throat muscles, but by the completest possible filling with breath of the breath-form and the resonance chambers, under the government of the controlling apparatus.

Neglect of the head tones (overtones) is paid for dearly.

The more violent exertions are made to force them, and to keep them, the worse are the results. For most of the unhappy singers who do this, there is but one result: the voice is lost. How pitiful!

If the first and second stages of tremolo are difficult to remedy, because the causes are rarely understood and the proper measures to take for their removal still more rarely, the repair of the last stage of the damage is nothing less than a fight, in which only an unspeakable patience can win the victory.

SECTION XXI

THE CURE

THERE are no magic cures for the singer. Only slowly, vibration upon vibration, can the true pitch be won back. In the word "soaring" lies the whole idea of the work. No more may the breath be allowed to flow uncontrolled through the wearied vocal cords; it must be forced against the chest, always, as if it were to come directly out thence. The throat muscles must lie fallow until they have lost the habit of cramped contraction; until the overtones again soar as they should, and are kept soaring long, though quite *piano*. At first this seems quite impossible, and is indeed very difficult, demanding all the patient's energy. But it is possible, and he cannot avoid it, for it is the only way to a thorough cure.

The patient has an extremely disagreeable period to pass through. If he is industrious and careful, he will soon find it impossible to sing in his old way; but the new way is for the most part quite unfamiliar to him, because his ear still hears as it has previously been accustomed to hear. It may be that years will pass before he can again use the muscles, so long maltreated. But he should not be dismayed at this prospect. If he can no longer use his voice in public as a singer, he certainly can as a teacher — for *a teacher must be able to sing well.* How should he describe to others sensations in singing which he himself never felt? Is it not as if he undertook to teach a language that he did not speak himself? or an instrument that he did not play himself? When he himself does not hear, how shall he teach others to hear?

The degree of the evil, and the patient's skill, naturally have much to do with the rapidity of the cure. But one cannot throw off a habit of years' standing like an old garment; and every new garment, too, is uncomfortable at first. One cannot expect an immediate cure, either of himself or of others. If the singer undertakes it with courage and energy, he learns to use his voice with conscious understanding, as should have been done in the beginning.

And he must make up his mind to it, that even after a good cure, the old habits will reappear, like corns in wet weather, whenever he is not in good form physically. That should not lead to discouragement; persistence will bring success.

As I have already said, singers with disabled voices like best to try "magic cures"; and there are teachers and pupils who boast of having effected such magic cures in a few weeks or hours.

Of them I give warning! and *equally*, of unprincipled physicians who daub around in the larynx, burn it, cut it, and make everything worse instead of better.

I cannot comprehend why singers do not unite to brand such people publicly and put an end to their doings once for all.

There is no other remedy than a slow, very careful study of the *causes* of the trouble, which in almost all cases consist in lack of control of the stream of breath through the vocal cords, and in disregard of the head tones, that is, of the over-tones; as well as in forcing the pitch and power of the tone upon a wrong resonating point of the palate, and in constricting the throat muscles. In these points almost invariably are all mistakes to be looked for; and in the recognition of them the proper means for correcting them are already indicated.

The cure is difficult and tedious. It needs an endless patience on the part of the sufferer as well as of the physician — that is, of the pupil and the *singing teacher* (the only proper physician for this disease) — because the nerves of the head are already sufficiently unstrung through the consciousness of their incapacity; yet they should be able to act easily and without effort in producing the head tones.

The repairing of a voice requires the greatest sympathetic appreciation and circumspection on the part of the teacher, who should always inspire the pupil with courage; and on the part of the pupil, all his tranquillity, nervous strength, and patience, in order to reach the desired goal.

Where there is a will there is a way!

SECTION XXII

THE TONGUE

SINCE it is the function of the tongue
to conduct the column of breath above the
larynx to the resonance chambers, too much
attention cannot be given to it and its position, in speaking as well as in singing. If it
lies too high or too low, it may, by constricting the breath, produce serious changes in
the tone, making it pinched or even shutting
it off entirely.

It has an extremely delicate and difficult
task to perform. It must be in such a position as not to press upon the larynx. Tongue
and larynx must keep out of each other's
way, although they always work in coöperation; but one must not hamper the other,
and when one can withdraw no farther
out of the way, the other must take it upon

itself to do so. For this reason the back of
the tongue must be raised high, the larynx
stand low.

The tongue must generally form a furrow.
With the lowest tones it lies relatively flattest, the tip *always* against and beneath the
front teeth, so that it can rise in the middle.

As soon as the furrow is formed, the mass
of the tongue is put out of the way, since it
stands high on both sides. It is almost impossible to make drawings of this; it can
best be seen in the mirror. As soon as the
larynx is low enough and the tongue set elastically against the palate and drawn up behind (see plate *a*), the furrow is formed of
itself. In pronouncing the vowel *ah* (which
must always be mixed with $\overline{oo}$ and *o*), it is a
good idea to think of yawning.

The furrow must be formed in order to
allow the breath to resonate against the palate beneath the nose, especially in the middle
range; that is, what a bass and a baritone
(whose highest range is not now under consid-

eration) would call their high range, all other
voices their middle.

Without the furrow in the tongue, no
tone is perfect in its resonance, none can
make full use of it.   The only exception is
the very highest head and falsetto tones,
which are without any palatal resonance and
have their place solely in the head cavities.
Strong and yet delicate, it must be able to
fit any letter of the alphabet; that is, help
form its sound.   It must be of the greatest
sensitiveness in adapting itself to every tonal
vibration, it must assist every change of
tone and letter as quick as a flash and with
unerring accuracy; without changing its position too soon or remaining too long in it,
in the highest range it must be able almost
to speak out in the air.

With all its strength and firmness this
furrow must be of the utmost sensitiveness
toward the breath, which, as I have often
said, must not be subjected to the least
pressure above the larynx or in the larynx

itself.   Pressure must be limited to the abdominal and chest muscles; and this might
better be called stress than pressure.

Without hindrance the column of breath,
at its upper end like diverging rays of light,
must fill and expand all the mucous membranes with its vibrations equally, diffuse
itself through the resonance chambers and
penetrate the cavities of the head.

When the back of the tongue can rise no
higher, the larynx must be lowered. This
often happens in the highest ranges, and one
needs only to mingle an *oo* in the vowel to
be sung, which must, however, be sounded
not forward in the mouth but *behind the nose*.
When the larynx must stand very low, the
tongue naturally must not be *too* high, else
it would affect the position of the larynx.
The mass of the tongue must then be disposed of elsewhere; that is, by the formation of a furrow (see plate).   One must learn
to feel and hear it.   To keep the larynx,
the back of the tongue, and the palate al-

ways in readiness to offer mutual assistance, must become a habit. I feel the interplay of tongue and larynx in my own case as shown in the plates.

As soon as we have the tongue under control, — that is, have acquired the habit of forming a furrow, — we can use it confidently as a support for the breath and the tone, and for vowels.

On its incurving back it holds firmly the vowels; with its tip, many of the consonants. With all its elasticity, it must be trained to great strength and endurance.

I, for instance, after every syllable, at once jerk my tongue with tremendous power back to its normal position in singing; that is, with its tip below the front teeth and the base raised ⌒. That goes on constantly, as quick as a flash. At the same time my larynx takes such a position that the tongue cannot interfere with it, that is, press upon it. By quickly raising the tongue toward the back, it is taken out of the way of the larynx, and the mass of the tongue is cleared from the throat. In the middle range, where the tongue or the larynx might be too high or too low, the furrow, which is of so much importance, is formed, in order to lead the vocalized breath first against the front of the palate beneath the nose, then slowly along the nose and behind it. Then when the highest point (the peak, which is extremely extensible) is reached, the pillars of the fauces are lowered, in order to leave the way for the head tones to the head cavities entirely free. In doing this, the sides of the tongue are raised high. Every tongue should occupy only so much space as it can occupy without being a hindrance to the tone.

The bad, bad tongue! one is too thick, another too thin, a third too long, a fourth much too short.

Ladies and gentlemen, these are nothing but the excuses of the lazy!

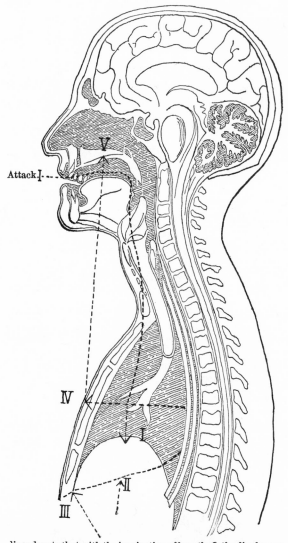

lines denote that with the inspiration of breath : I, the diaphragm
is sensibly stretched backward ; II, enlarges the capacity of
the chest by the drawing down of its floor ; III, and so forms
the supply chamber for the breath ; IV, indicates the pressure
of the breath against the chest tension muscles ; V, the attack

SECTION XXIII

PREPARATION FOR SINGING

No one can sing properly without first preparing for it, mentally and physically, with all the organs concerned in the production of the voice.

We have in this to perform three functions, simultaneously : —

First, to draw breath quietly, not too deeply ; to force the breath against the chest and hold it there firmly till the upward and outward streaming — that is, singing — begins. (See plate, The Path of the Breath.)

Second, to raise the soft palate at the same time toward the nose, so that the breath remains stationary until the singing begins.

Third, to jerk the tongue backward at the same time, its back being thus raised, and elastic, ready to meet all the wishes of the singer, — that is, the needs of the larynx. The larynx must not be pressed either too low or too high, but must work freely. The breath is enabled to stream forth from it like a column, whose form is moulded above the larynx by the base of the tongue.

When these three functions have been performed, all is ready. Now the pitch of the tone is to be considered, as the singing begins.

The consummation (Höhepunkt) of the tone, above the palate, gives the point of attack itself, under the palate.

Now further care must be given that the point of attack on the palate — that is, the focal point of the breath — be not subjected to pressure, and that the entire supply of breath be not expended upon the palatal resonance.

For this the palate must remain elastic, for it has a twofold duty to perform. It must not only furnish resistance for the focal

point of the breath, — except in the very
highest head tones, — around which it can be
diffused ; the same resistance, which stands
against the stream of breath from below,
must also afford a firm, pliant, and elastic
floor for the overtones, which, soaring above
the palate, shift, as is needed, to or above the
hard and soft palate, or are divided in the
nose, forehead, and head cavities.   It can
easily be seen how any pressure in singing
can be dangerous everywhere, and how careful the singer is forced to be to avoid such
mistakes.

SECTION XXIV·

THE POSITION OF THE MOUTH (CONTRACTION OF THE MUSCLES OF SPEECH)

WHAT must my sensations be with the muscles of speech? How shall I control them?

The best position of the mouth, the means of securing the proper use of the muscles of speech and of the vocal organs, is established by pronouncing the vowel $\bar{a}$, not too sharply, in the middle range of the voice, and trying to retain the position of the muscles after the sound has ceased.

This cannot be done without a *smiling* position of the mouth, consequently with a strong contraction of the muscles of the mouth, tongue, and throat, which can be felt to be drawn up as far as the ears.

In doing so the tongue — as far as the tip

— lies of a pretty nearly even height to the back ⌐, the soft palate soars without arching, but rather somewhat depressed over it.

In pronouncing the vowels $\bar{a}$ and $\bar{e}$, the bright vowels, the full stream of the breath, in the given position, can only partly pass between the tongue and the palate. The other part is forced — unless the larynx stands too high and can choke it off — above the palate into the nasal cavities, to seek its opportunity for resonance.

The path for $\bar{a}$ and $\bar{e}$ above the palate is worthy of all attention as a place for the overtones of the middle voice. If the soft palate, in the lower middle tones, is forced too far toward the hard palate, the covered tones are without vibrancy. One must needs secure the help of the nose especially, when the palate is sunk beneath the nose, by inflating the nostrils and letting air stream in and out of them.

I repeat the warning, not to force several tones upon the same resonating point, but to see that upon each tone the form necessary for succeeding tones is prepared. Neglect of this will sooner or later be paid for dearly.

Notwithstanding the strong muscular contraction that the vocal organs must undergo in pronouncing the vowel $\bar{a}$, the breath must be able to flow gently and without hindrance through its form, in order completely to fill up its resonance chambers.   Again, and always, attention must be given that in singing, and in speaking as well, nothing shall be cramped or held tense, except the pressure of the breath against the chest.   It is of the utmost importance to maintain this position for *all* vowels, with the least possible perceptible modifications.

How can this be done?   *A* and *e* are bright vowels, must be sung with a pleasant, almost smiling, position of the mouth.   *U* and *o*, on the contrary, are dark vowels, for

which the lips must be drawn into a sort
of spout.   Look at the position of the throat
in these vowels : (1) as they are usually sung
and spoken ; (2) as I feel it, in singing, as
I sing them, and as they must be sung and
felt.

SECTION XXV

CONNECTION OF VOWELS

How do I connect them with each other? If I wish to connect closely together two vowels that lie near to or far from each other, I must first establish the muscular contractions for $\bar{a}$, and introduce between the two vowels, whether they lie near together or far apart, a very well-defined y.   Then (supposing, for instance, that I want to connect $\bar{a}$ and $\bar{e}$) I must join the $\bar{a}$ closely to the y, and the y closely to the e, so that there is not the least resonating space between the two that is not filled during the changes in the position of the organs, however carefully this is undertaken.   There must be no empty space, no useless escape of breath, between any two of the sounds.

At first only two, then three and four, and

I

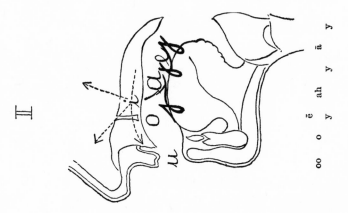

oo ē ˘o ā ah

II

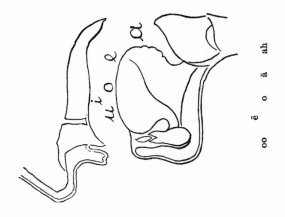

oo o ē ah y ā y
      y   y

I

Bad.

oo   ē   o   ā   ah

II

Good.

oo   o   ē   ah   ā

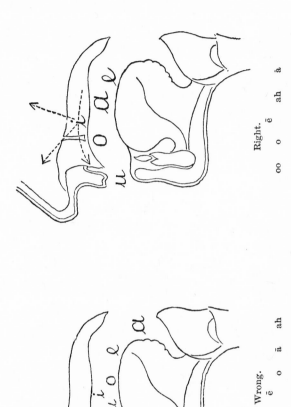

I

Wrong.

ē o ā ah

oo o ā ah

II

Right.

ē ē ah ă

oo o ē ah ă

then all the vowels in succession must be so practised : —

A-ye, a-ye-yu, a-ye-yoo-yü, a-ye-yo-yü-yu-ye-yah.

But there must be never more than so much breath at hand as is needed to make the vowel and the tone perfect. The more closely the vowels are connected with the help of the *y*, the less breath is emitted from the mouth unused, the more intimate is the connection of tone, and the less noticeable are the changes of the position of the organs in relation to each other.

When I pass from *yā-yē* to *yoo*, I am compelled to develop very strongly the muscular contraction of the lips, which are formed into a long projecting spout; and this movement cannot be sufficiently exaggerated. With every new *y* I must produce renewed muscular contractions of the vocal organs, which gradually, through continuous practice, are trained to become almost like the finest, most pliable steel, upon which the fullest reliance

may be placed. From *yoo* it is best to go to
yü, that lies still farther forward and requires
of the lips an iron firmness; then to *yo*, touching slightly on the *e* that lies above the *o*;
then return to *yā*, and not till then going to
ye-ah, which must then feel thus: —

e
oo-o ah-ā
y

The *y* is taken under the *ah*, that the word
may not slide under; for usually the thought
of *ah* relaxes all the organs: the tongue lies
flat, the larynx becomes unsteady, is without
definite position, and the palate is not arched
and is without firmness. In this way *ah* becomes the most colorless and empty vowel of
the whole list.

With every change of vowel, or of any
other letter, there are changes in the position of the organs, since tongue, palate, and
larynx must take different positions for different sounds.

With *ā* and *ē* the larynx stands higher, the
palate is sunk, or in its normal position.

With *oo*, *o*, and *ah* the larynx stands low,
the palate is arched.

With *a*, *e*, and *ah* the lips are drawn back.

With *oo*, *o*, *ü*, and *ö* they are extended far
forward.

The auxiliary sound *y* connects them all
with each other, so that the transitions are
made quite imperceptibly. Since it is pronounced with the tongue drawn high against
the palate, it prevents the base of the tongue
from falling down again.

This should be practised very slowly, that
the sensations may be clearly discerned, and
that no vibration that gives the vowel its
pitch and duration may escape attention.

The muscular contraction described com-
prises the chief functions of the vocal organs,
and is as necessary for singing as the breath
is for the tone. Year in and year out every
singer and pupil must practise it in daily
exercises as much as possible, on every tone
of the vocal compass.

In the lowest as well as in the highest

range the sharpness of the *a* is lost, as well as the clear definition of all single vowels. *A* should be mingled with *oo*, *ah*, and *e*. In the highest range, the vowels are merged in each other, because then the principal thing is not the vowel, but the high sound.

Even the *thought* of *ā* and *ē*, the latter especially, raises the pitch of the tone. The explanation of this is that *ā* and *ē* possess sympathetic sounds above the palate that lead the breath to the resonance of the head cavities.

For this reason tenors often, in high notes. resort to the device of changing words with dark vowels to words with the bright vowel *e*. They could attain the same end, without changing the whole word, by simply *thinking* of an *e*.

Without over-exertion, the singer can practise the exercises given above twenty times a day, in periods of ten to fifteen minutes each, and will soon appreciate the advantage of the muscular strengthening they

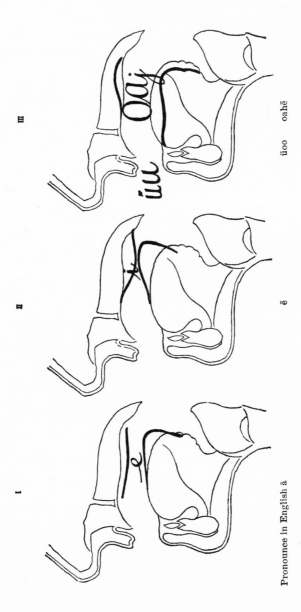

I   II   III

Pronounce in English ā   ē   ĭoo   oahē

give. They make the voice fresh, not
weary, as doubtless many will suppose.

What, then, can be expected of an untrained organ? Nothing!

Without daily vocal gymnastics no power
of endurance in the muscles can be gained.
They must be so strong that a great operatic rôle can be repeated ten times in succession, in order that the singer may become
able to endure the strain of singing in opera
houses, in great auditoriums, and make
himself heard above a great orchestra, without suffering for it.

When I, for instance, was learning the
part of *Isolde*, I could without weariness
sing the first act alone six times in succession, with expression, action, and a full
voice. That was my practice with all my
rôles. After I had rehearsed a rôle a thousand times in my own room, I would go
into the empty theatre and rehearse single
scenes, as well as the whole opera, for hours
at a time. That gave me the certainty of

being mistress of my resonances down to the last note; and very often I felt able to begin it all over again. So must it be, if one wishes to accomplish anything worth while.

Another end also is attained by the same exercise, — the connection, not only of the vowels, but of all letters, syllables, words, and phrases. By this exercise the form for the breath, tone, and word, in which all the organs are adjusted to each other with perfect elasticity, is gradually established. Slowly but surely it assures greatest endurance in all the organs concerned in speaking and singing, the inseparable connection of the palatal resonance with the resonance of the head cavities. In this way is gained perfection in the art of singing, which is based, not on chance, but on knowledge; and this slow but sure way is the only way to gain it.

By the above-described method all other alphabetical sounds can be connected, and exercises can be invented to use with it, which are best adapted to correct the mistakes of pupils, at first on one, then step by step on two and three connected tones, etc.

At the same time it is necessary to learn to move the tongue freely, and with the utmost quickness, by jerking it back, after pronouncing consonants, as quick as a flash, into the position in which it conducts the breath to the resonating chambers for the vowels.   With all these movements is connected the power of elastically contracting and relaxing the muscles.

SECTION XXVI

THE LIPS

OF special importance for the tone and the word are the movements of the lips, which are so widely different in the bright and in the dark vowels. These movements cannot be too much exaggerated in practising. The same strength and elasticity to which we have to train the muscles of the throat and tongue must be imparted to the lips, which must be as of iron. Upon their coöperation much of the life of the tone depends, and it can be used in many shadings, as soon as one is able to exert their power consciously and under the control of the will.

Every vowel, every word, every tone, can be colored as by magic in all sorts of ways by the well-controlled play of the lips; can, as it were, be imbued with life, as the lips open or close more or less in different positions. The lips are the final cup-shaped resonators through which the tone has to pass. They can retard it or let it escape, can color it bright or dark, and exert a ceaseless and ever varying influence upon it long before it ceases and up to its very end.

No attempt should be made to use the play of the lips until complete mastery of the absolutely even, perfect tone, and of the muscular powers, has been acquired. The effect must be produced as a result of power and practice; and should not be practised as an effect *per se*.

SECTION XXVII

THE VOWEL-SOUND *AH*

THERE is much discussion as to whether *ah*, *oo*, or some other vowel is the one best adapted for general practice. In former times practice was entirely on the vowel-sound *ah*. The old Italians taught it; my mother was trained so, and never allowed her pupils to use any other vowel during the first months of their instruction. Later, to be sure, every letter, every word, was practised and improved continually, till it was correct, and had impressed itself upon the memory, as well as the ear, of the pupil for all time.

I explain the matter thus: —

The singer's mouth should always make an agreeable impression. Faces that are forever grinning or showing fish mouths are disgusting and wrong.

The pleasing expression of the mouth requires the muscular contractions that form the bright vowel *ah*.

Most people who are not accustomed to using their vocal resonance pronounce the *ah* quite flat, as if it were the vowel-sound lying lowest. If it is pronounced with the position of the mouth belonging to the bright vowels, it has to seek its resonance, in speaking as well as in singing, in the same place as the dark vowels, on the high-arched palate. To permit this, it must be mingled with *oo*. The furrows in the tongue must also be formed, just as with *oo* and *o*, only special attention must be given that the back of the tongue does not fall, but remains high, as in pronouncing *ā*. In this way *ah* comes to lie between *oo-o'ah'yā*, and forms at the same time the connection between the bright and the dark vowels, and the reverse.

For this reason it was proper that *ah* should be preferred as the practice vowel, as soon as it was placed properly between

the two extremes, and had satisfied all demands.   I prefer to teach it, because its
use makes all mistakes most clearly recog-
nizable. It is the most difficult vowel. If
it is well pronounced, or sung, it produces
the necessary muscular contractions with a
pleasing expression of the mouth, and makes
certain a fine tone color by its connection
with *oo* and *o*. If the *ah* is equally well
formed in all ranges of the voice, a chief
difficulty is mastered.

Those who have been badly taught, or
have fallen into bad ways, should practise
the vocal exercise I have given above, with
ya-ye-yah, etc., slowly, listening to themselves
carefully.   Good results cannot fail; it is
an infallible means of improvement.

Italians who sing well never speak or
sing the vowel sound *ah* otherwise than
mixed, and only the neglect of this mixture
could have brought about the decadence of
the Italian teaching of song. In Germany
no attention is paid to it. The *ah*, as sung

generally by most Italians of the present day, quite flat, sounds commonplace, almost like an affront. It can range itself, that is connect itself, with no other vowel, makes all vocal connection impossible, evolves very ugly registers; and, lying low in the throat, summons forth no palatal resonance. The power of contraction of the muscles of speech is insufficient, and this insufficiency misleads the singer to constrict the throat muscles, which are not trained to the endurance of it; thereby further progress is made impossible. In the course of time the tone becomes flat at the transitions. The fatal tremolo is almost always the result of this manner of singing.

Try to sing a scale upward on *ah*, placing the tongue and muscles of speech at the same time on *ā*, and you will be surprised at the agreeable effect. Even the thought of it alone is often enough, because the tongue involuntarily takes the position of its own accord.

I remember very well how Mme. Désirée
Artot-Padilla, who had a low mezzo-soprano
voice, used to toss off great coloratura pieces,
beginning on the vowel-sound *ah*, and then
going up and down on *a, ee, aüoah*.   At
the time I could not understand why she
did it; now I know perfectly, — because it
was easier for her.   The breath is impelled
against the cavities of the head, the head
tones are set into action.

Behind the *a* position there must be as
much room provided as is needed for all the
vowels, with such modifications as each one
requires for itself.   The matter of chief importance is the position of the tongue *in*
the throat, that it shall not be in the way
of the larynx, which must be able to move
up and down, even though very slightly,
without hindrance.

All vowels must be able to flow into each
other; the singer must be able to pass from
one to another without perceptible alteration,
and back again.

SECTION XXVIII

ITALIAN AND GERMAN

How easy it is for the Italians, who have by nature, through the characteristics of their native language, all these things which others must gain by long years of practice! A single syllable often unites three vowels; for instance, " tuoi " (tuoyē), " miei " (myeayē), " muoja," etc.

The Italians mingle all their vowels. They rub them into and color them with each other. This includes a great portion of the art of song, which in every language, with due regard to its peculiar characteristics, must be learned by practice.

To give only a single example of the difficulty of the German words, with the everlasting consonant endings to the syllables, take the recitative at the entrance of Norma: —

"Wer lässt hier Aufruhrstimmen, Kriegs-
ruf ertönen, wollt Ihr die Götter zwingen,
Eurem Wahnwitz zu fröhnen? Wer wagt
vermessen, gleich der Prophetin der Zukunft
Nacht zu lichten, wollt Ihr der Götter Plan
vorschnell vernichten? Nicht Menschenkraft
Können die Wirren dieses Landes schlichten."

Twelve endings on n!

"Sediziosi voci, voci di guerra, avoi chi
alzar si attenta presso all' ara del Dio! V'ha
chi presume dettar responsi alla vegente
Norma, e di Roma affrettar il fato arcano.
Ei non dipende, no, non dipende da potere
umano!"

From the Italians we can learn the connection of the vowels, from the French the use
of the nasal tone. The Germans surpass the
others in their power of expressiveness. But
he who would have the right to call himself
an artist must unite all these things; the *bel
canto*, that is, beautiful — I might say good —
singing, and all the means of expression
which we cultivated people need to interpret

master works of great minds, should afford
the public ennobling pleasure.

A tone full of life is to be produced only
by the skilful mixture of the vowels, that is,
the unceasing leaning of one upon the others,
without, however, affecting any of its characteristics. This means, in reality, only the
complete use of the resonance of the breath,
since the mixture of the vowels can be obtained only through the elastic conjunction
of the organs and the varying division of the
stream of breath toward the palatal resonance, or that of the cavities of the head, or
the equalization of the two.

The larynx must rise and descend unimpeded by the tongue, soft palate and pillars
of the fauces rise and sink, the soft palate
always able more or less to press close to the
hard. Strong and elastic contractions imply
very pliable and circumspect relaxation of the
same.

I think that the feeling I have of the extension of my throat comes from the very

powerful yet very elastic contraction of my muscles, which, though feeling always in a state of relaxability, appear to me like flexible steel, of which I can demand everything, — because never too much, — and which I exercise daily. Even in the entr'actes of grand operas I go through with such exercises; for they refresh instead of exhausting me.

The unconstrained coöperation of all the organs, as well as their individual functions, must go on elastically without any pressure or cramped action. Their interplay must be powerful yet supple, that the breath which produces the tone may be diffused as it flows from one to another of the manifold and complicated organs (such as the ventricles of Morgagni), supporting itself on others, being caught in still others, and finding all in such a state of readiness as is required in each range for each tone. Everything must be combined in the right way as a matter of habit.

The voice is equalized by the proper ramification of the breath and the proper connection of the different resonances.

The tone is colored by the proper mixture of vowels; *oo*, *o*, and *ah* demanding more palatal resonance and a lower position of the larynx, *a* and *e* more resonance of the head cavities and a higher position of the larynx. With *oo*, *o*, *ü*, and *ah* the palate is arched higher (the tongue forming a furrow) than with *ā*, *ē*, and *ü*, where the tongue lies high and flat.

There are singers who place the larynx too low, and, arching the palate too high, sing too much toward *oo*. Such voices sound very dark, perhaps even hollow; they lack the interposition of the *ā*, — that is, the larynx is placed too low.

On the other hand, there are others who press it upward too high; their *a* position is a permanent one. Such voices are marked by a very bright, sharp quality of tone, often like a goat's bleating.

Both are alike wrong and disagreeable.

The proper medium between them must be gained by sensitive training of the ear, and a taste formed by the teacher through examples drawn from his own singing and that of others.

If we wish to give a noble expression to the tone and the word, we must mingle its vocal sound, if it is not so, with *o* or *oo*. If we wish to give the word merely an agreeable expression, we mingle it with *ah*, *ā*, and *ē*. That is, we must use all the qualities of tonal resonance, and thus produce colors which shall benefit the tone and thereby the word and its expression.

Thus a single tone may be taken or sung in many different ways. In every varying connection, consequently, the singer must be able to change it according to the expression desired. But as soon as it is a question of a *musical phrase*, in which several tones or words, or tones alone, are connected, the law of progression must remain in force; expression must be sacrificed, partly at least, to the beauty of the musical passage.

If he is skilful enough, the singer can impart a certain expression of feeling to even the most superficial phrases and coloratura passages. Thus, in the coloratura passages of Mozart's arias, I have always sought to gain expressiveness by *crescendi*, choice of significant points for breathing, and breaking off of phrases. I have been especially successful with this in the *Entführung*, introducing a tone of lament into the first aria, a heroic dignity into the second, through the coloratura passages. Without exaggerating petty details, the artist must exploit all the means of expression that he is justified in using.

SECTION XXIX

AUXILIARY VOWELS

LIKE the auxiliary verbs "will" and "have," $\bar{a}$, $\bar{e}$, and oo are auxiliary vowels, of whose aid we are constantly compelled to avail ourselves. It will perhaps sound exaggerated when I present an example of this, but as a matter of fact pronunciation is consummated in this way; only, it must not become noticeable. The method seems singular, but its object is to prevent the leaving of any empty resonance space, and to obviate any interruptions that could affect the perfection of the tone.

For example, when I wish to sing the word "Fräulein," I must first, and before all else, think of the pitch of the tone, before I attack the f. With the f, the tone must be there already, *before* I have pronounced it; to pass

from the *f* to the *r* I must summon to my aid
the auxiliary vowel *oo*, in order to prevent the

formation of any unvocalized interstices in
the sound.   The *r* must not now drop off, but
must in turn be joined to the *oo*, while the
tongue should not drop down behind,
but should complete the vibrations thus,
in a straight line.   (See plate.)

It is very interesting to note how much
a word can gain or lose in fulness and beauty
of tone.   Without the use of auxiliary vowels
no connection of the resonance in words can
be effected; there is then no beautiful tone
in singing, only a kind of hacking.   Since it
must be quite imperceptible, the use of auxiliary vowels must be very artistically managed, and is best practised in the beginning
very slowly on single tones and words, then
proceeding with great care to two tones, two

syllables, and so on. In this way the pupil learns to *hear*. But he must learn to hear very slowly and for a long time, until there is no failure of vibration in the tone and word, and it is all so impressed upon his memory that it can never be lost. The auxiliary vowels must always be present, but the listener should be able to hear, from the assistance of the *oo*, only the warmth and nobility of the tone, from the *a* and *e* only the carrying power and brilliancy of it.

SECTION XXX

K, l, m, n, p, s, and *r* at the end of a word or syllable must be made resonant by joining to the end of the word or syllable a rather audible *ĕ (eh)*; for instance, Wandel ᵉ, Gretel ᵉ, etc.

A thing that no one teaches any longer, or knows or is able to do, a thing that only Betz and I knew, and with me will probably disappear entirely, is the dividing and ending of syllables that must be effected under certain conditions. It may have originated with the Italian school.

I was taught it especially upon double consonants. When two come together, they must be divided; the first, as in Him-mel, being sounded dull, and without resonance, the syllable and tone being kept as nasal as

229

possible, the lips closed, and a pause being
made between the two syllables; not till then
is the second syllable pronounced, with a new
formation of the second consonant.

And this is done, not only in case of a
doubling of one consonant, but whenever two
consonants come together to close the syllable; for instance, win-ter, dring-en, kling-en,
bind-en; in these the nasal sound plays a
specially important part.

The tediousness of singing without proper
separation of the syllables is not appreciated
till it has been learned how to divide the consonants. The nasal close of itself brings a
new color into the singing, which must be
taken into account; and moreover, the word
is much more clearly intelligible, especially in
large auditoriums, where an appreciable length
of time is needed for it to reach the listener.
By the nasal close, also, an uninterrupted
connection is assured between the consonant
and the tone, even if the latter has to cease,
apparently, for an instant.

I teach all my pupils thus. But since most of them consider it something unheard of to be forced to pronounce in this way, they very rarely bring it to the artistic perfection which alone can make it effective. Except from Betz, I have never heard it from any one. After me no one will teach it any more. I shall probably be the last one. A pity!

SECTION XXXI

PRACTICAL EXERCISES

THE practical study of singing is best begun with single sustained tones, and with preparation on the sound of *ah* alone, mingled with *o* and *oo*. A position as if one were about to yawn helps the tongue to lie in the right place.

In order not to weary young voices too much, it is best to begin in the middle range, going upward first, by semitones, and then, starting again with the same tone, going downward. All other exercises begin in the lower range and go upward.

The pupil must first be able to make a single tone good, and judge it correctly, before he should be allowed to proceed to a second. Later, single syllables or words can be used as exercises for this.

The position of the mouth and tongue must be watched in the mirror. The vowel *ah* must be mingled with *o* and *oo*, and care must be taken that the breath is forced strongly against the chest, and felt attacking here and on the palate at the same time. Begin *piano*, make a long *crescendo*, and gradually return and end on a well-controlled *piano*. My feeling at the attack is as shown in the plate.

At the same instant that I force the breath against the chest, I place the tone *under* its highest point on the palate, and let the over-tones soar above the palate — the two united in one thought. Only in the lowest range can the overtones, and in the highest range the undertones (resonance of the head cavities and of the palate), be dispensed with.

With me the throat never comes into con-sideration; I feel absolutely nothing of it, at most only the breath gently streaming through it. A tone should never be forced; *never press* the breath against the resonating chambers, but only against the chest; and NEVER hold it back. The organs should not be cramped, but should be allowed to perform their functions elastically.

The contraction of the muscles should never exceed their power to relax. A tone must always be sung, whether strong or soft, with an easy, conscious power. Further, before all things, sing always with due regard to the pitch.

In this way the control of the ear is exercised over the pitch, strength, and duration of the tone, and over the singer's strength and weakness, of which we are often forced to make a virtue. In short, one learns to recognize and to produce a perfect tone.

In all exercises go as low and as high as the voice will allow without straining, and always make little pauses to rest between them, even if you are not tired, in order to be all the fresher for the next one. With a certain amount of skill and steady purpose the voice increases its compass, and takes the

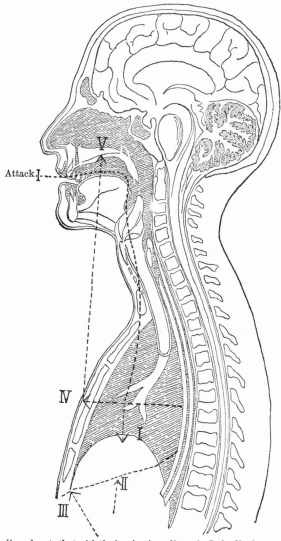

Attack.I.

V

IV

I

II

III

lines denote that with the inspiration of breath : J, the diaphragm
is sensibly stretched backward ; II, enlarges the capacity of
the chest by the drawing down of its floor ; III, and so forms
the supply chamber for the breath ; IV, indicates the pressure
of the breath against the chest tension muscles ; V, the attack

proper range, easiest to it by nature. The
pupil can see then how greatly the compass of a voice can be extended. For
amateurs it is not necessary; but it is for
every one who practises the profession of a
singer in public.

For a second exercise, sing connectedly
two half-tones, slowly, on one or two vowels,
bridging them with the auxiliary vowels and
the *y* as the support of the tongue, etc.

Every tone must seek its best results
from all the organs concerned in its production; must possess power, brilliancy, and
mellowness in order to be able to produce,
before leaving each tone, the propagation
form for the next tone, ascending as well as
descending, and make it certain.

No exercise should be dropped till every
vibration of every tone has clearly approved
itself to the ear, not only of the teacher,
but also of the pupil, as *perfect*.

It takes a long time to reach the full
consciousness of a tone. After it has passed

the lips it must be diffused outside, before it
can come to the consciousness of the listener
as well as to that of the singer himself.   So
practise *singing* slowly. and *hearing* slowly.

SECTION XXXII

THE GREAT SCALE

THIS is the most necessary exercise for all kinds of voices. It was taught to my mother; she taught it to all her pupils and to us. But *I* am probably the only one of them all who practises it faithfully! I do not trust the others. As a pupil one must practise it twice a day, as a professional singer at least once.

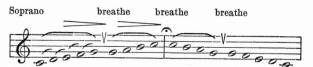

The breath must be well prepared, the expiration still better, for the duration of these five and four long tones is greater than would be supposed. The first tone must be attacked not too *piano*, and sung only so strongly as is necessary to reach the next

239

one easily without further crescendo, while the propagation form for the next tone is produced, and the breath wisely husbanded till the end of the phrase.

The first of each of the phrases ends nasally in the middle range, the second toward the forehead and the cavities of the head. The lowest tone must already be prepared to favor the resonance of the head cavities, by thinking of $\bar{a}$, consequently placing the larynx high and maintaining the resonating organs in a *very* supple and elastic state. In the middle range, *ah* is mingled particularly with *oo*, that the nose may be reached; further, the auxiliary vowel *e* is added to it, which guides the tone to the head cavities. In descending the attack must be more concentrated, as the tone is slowly directed toward the nose on *oo* or *o*, to the end of the figure.

When *oo*, *a*, and *e* are auxiliary vowels, they need not be plainly pronounced. (They form an exception in the diphthongs,

" Trauuum," " Leiiid," " Lauuune," " Feuyer,"
etc.) As auxiliary vowels they are only
means to an end, a bridge, a connection
from one thing to another. They can be
taken anywhere with any other sound; and
thence it may be seen how elastic the organs
can be when they are skilfully managed.

The chief object of the great scale is to
secure the pliant, sustained use of the breath,
precision in the preparation of the propagation form, the proper mixture of the vowels
which aid in placing the organs in the right
position for the tone, to be changed for every
different tone, although imperceptibly; further,
the intelligent use of the resonance of the
palate and head cavities, especially the latter,
whose tones, soaring above everything else,
form the connection with the nasal quality for
the whole scale.

The scale must be practised without too
strenuous exertion, but not without power,
gradually extending over the entire compass
of the voice; and that is, if it is to be per-

fect, over a compass of two octaves. These two octaves will have been covered, when, advancing the starting-point by semitones, the scale has been carried up through an entire octave. So much every voice can finally accomplish, even if the high notes must be very feeble.

The great scale, properly elaborated in practice, accomplishes wonders: it equalizes the voice, makes it flexible and noble, gives strength to all weak places, operates to repair all faults and breaks that exist, and controls the voice to the very heart. Nothing escapes it.

By it ability as well as inability is brought to light — something that is extremely unpleasant to those without ability. In my opinion it is the ideal exercise, but the most difficult one I know. By devoting forty minutes to it every day, a consciousness of certainty and strength will be gained that ten hours a day of any other exercise cannot give.

This should be the chief test in all conser-

vatories. If I were at the head of one, the
pupils should be allowed for the first three
years to sing at the examinations only *difficult* exercises, like this great scale, before they
should be allowed to think of singing a song
or an aria, which I regard only as cloaks for
incompetency.

For teaching me this scale — this guardian
angel of the voice — I cannot be thankful
enough to my mother. In earlier years I
used to like to express myself freely about
it. There was a time when I imagined that
it strained me. My mother often ended her
warnings at my neglect of it with the words,
" You will be very sorry for it ! " And I was
very sorry for it. At one time, when I was
about to be subjected to great exertions, and
did not practise it every day, but thought it
was enough to sing coloratura fireworks, I
soon became aware that my transition tones
would no longer endure the strain, began
easily to waver, or threatened even to become too flat. The realization of it was terri-

ble! It cost me many, many years of the hardest and most careful study; and it finally brought me to realize the necessity of exercising the vocal organs continually, and in the proper way, if I wished always to be able to rely on them.

Practice, and especially the practice of the great, slow scale, is the only cure for all injuries, and at the same time the most excellent means of fortification against all over-exertion. I sing it every day, often twice, even if I have to sing one of the greatest rôles in the evening. I can rely absolutely on its assistance.

If I had imparted nothing else to my pupils but the ability to sing this one great exercise well, they would possess a capital fund of knowledge which must infallibly bring them a rich return on their voices. I often take fifty minutes to go through it only once, for I let no tone pass that is lacking in any degree in pitch, power, and duration, or in a single vibration of the propagation form.

SECTION XXXIII

VELOCITY

SINGERS, male and female, who are lacking velocity and the power of trilling, seem to me like horses without tails. Both of these things belong to the art of song, and are inseparable from it. It is a matter of indifference whether the singer has to use them or not; he must be able to. The teacher who neither teaches nor can teach them to his pupils is a *bad teacher;* the pupil who, notwithstanding the urgent warnings of his teacher, neglects the exercises that can help him to acquire them, and fails to perfect himself in them, is a *bungler.* There is no excuse for it but lack of talent, or laziness; and neither has any place in the higher walks of art.

To give the voice velocity, practise first slowly, then faster and faster, figures of

five, six, seven, and eight notes, etc., upward and downward.

If one has well mastered the great, slow
scale, with the nasal connection, skill in singing rapid passages will be developed quite
of itself, because they both rest on the same
foundation, and without the preliminary practice can never be understood.

Put the palate into the nasal position, the
larynx upon *œ*; attack the lowest tone of the
figure with the thought of the highest; force
the breath, as it streams very vigorously forth
from the larynx, toward the nose, but allow
the head current entire freedom, without entirely doing away with the nasal quality; and
then run up the scale with great firmness.

In descending, keep the form of the
highest tone, even if there should be eight
to twelve tones in the passage, so that the
scale slides down, not a pair of stairs, but a
smooth track, the highest tone affording, as
it were, a guarantee that on the way there
shall be no impediment or sudden drop.

The resonance form, kept firm and tense, must adapt itself with the utmost freedom to the thought of every tone, and with it, to the breath. The pressure of the breath against the chest must not be diminished, but must be unceasing.

To me it is always as if the pitch of the highest tone were already contained in the lowest, so strongly concentrated upon the whole figure are my thoughts at the attack of a single tone. By means of *ah-e-ā*, larynx, tongue, and palatal position on the lowest tone are in such a position that the vibrations of breath for the highest tones are already finding admission into the head cavities, and as far as possible are in sympathetic vibration there.

The higher the vocal figures go the more breath they need, the less can the breath and the organs be pressed. The higher they are, the more breath must stream forth from the epiglottis; therefore the *ā* and the thought of *e*, which keep the passages to

the head open.   But because there is a limit
to the scope of the movement of larynx and
tongue, and they cannot rise higher and
higher with a figure that often reaches to
an immense height, the singer must resort
to the aid of the auxiliary vowel *oo*, in
order to lower the larynx and so make
room for the breath :

A run or any other figure must never
sound thus :

but must be nasally modified above, and
tied ; and because the breath must flow out
unceasingly in a powerful stream from the
vocal cords, an *h* can only be put in beneath,
which makes us sure of this powerful streaming out of the breath, and helps only the

branch stream of breath into the cavities of the head. Often singers hold the breath, concentrated on the nasal form, firmly on the lowest tone of a figure, and, without interrupting this nasal form, or the head tones, that is, the breath vibrating in the head cavities, finish the figure alone. When this happens the muscular contractions of the throat, tongue, and palate are very strong.

L'oiselet. Chopin-Viardat

The turn, too, based on the consistent connection of the tonal figure with the nasal quality, — which is obtained by pronouncing the *oo* toward the nose, — and firmly held there, permits no interruption for an instant to the vowel sound.

How often have I heard the *ha-ha-ha-haa*,

etc., — a wretched tumbling down of different
tones, instead of a smooth decoration of the
cantilena.   Singers generally disregard it,
because no one can do it any more, and yet
even to-day it is of the greatest importance.
(See *Tristan und Isolde*.)

The situation is quite the same in regard to
the appoggiatura.   In this the resonance is
made nasal and the flexibility of the larynx,
— which, without changing the resonance,
moves quickly up and down — accomplishes
the task alone.   Here, too, it can almost be
imagined that the *thought* alone is enough,
for the connection of the two tones cannot
be too close.   But this must be practised, and
done *consciously*.

Adelaide, by Beethoven

A - bend - lüft - chen im   zar-ten L'au-be flü-stern

SECTION XXXIV

TRILL

THERE still remains the trill, which is best practised in the beginning as follows : —

The breath is led very far back against the head cavities by the $\bar{a}$, the larynx kept as stiff as possible and placed high. Both tones are connected as closely, as heavily as possible, upward nasally, downward *on* the larynx, for which the y, again, is admirably suited. They must be attacked as high as possible, and very strongly. The trill exercise must be practised almost as a scream.

The upper note must always be strongly
accented. The exercise is practised with an
even strength, without decrescendo to the
end; the breath streams out more and more
strongly, uninterruptedly to the finish.

Trill exercises must be performed with
great energy, on the whole compass of the
voice. They form an exception to the rule
in so far that in them more is given to
the throat to do — always, however, under
the control of the chest — than in other
exercises. That relates, however, to the
muscles.

The breath vibrates *above* the larynx, but
does not stick in it, consequently this is not
dangerous.

The exercise is practised first on two half,
then on two whole, tones of the same key
(as given above), advancing by semitones,
twice a day on the entire compass of the
voice. It is exhausting because it requires
great energy; but for the same reason it
gives strength. Practise it first as slowly

and vigorously as the strength of the throat allows, then faster and faster, till one day the trill unexpectedly appears. With some energy and industry good results should be reached in from six to eight weeks, and the larynx should take on the habit of performing its function by itself. This function gradually becomes a habit, so that it seems as if only *one* tone were attacked and held, and as if the second tone simply vibrated with it. As a matter of fact, the larynx will have been so practised in the minute upward and downward motion, that the singer is aware only of the vibrations of the breath that lie *above* it, while he remains mindful all the time only of the pitch of the upper note.

One has the feeling then as of singing or holding only the *lower* tone (which must be placed very high), while the upper one vibrates with it simply through the habitude of the accentuation. The union of the two then comes to the singer's consciousness as

if he were singing the lower note somewhat too high, halfway toward the upper
one. This is only an aural delusion, produced by the high vibrations. But the
trill, when fully mastered, should always
be begun, as in the exercise, on the *upper*
note.

Every voice must master the trill, after a
period, longer or shorter, of proper practice.
Stiff, strong voices master it sooner than
small, weak ones. I expended certainly ten
years upon improving it, because as a young
girl I had so very little strength, although
my voice was very flexible in executing all
sorts of rapid passages.

To be able to use it anywhere, of course,
requires a long time and much practice.
For this reason it is a good plan to practise
it on syllables with different vowels, such as
can all be supported on $\bar{a}$, and on words, as
soon as the understanding needed for this
is in some degree assured.

If the larynx has acquired the habit

properly, the trill can be carried on into a *piano* and *pianissimo* and prolonged almost without end with *crescendi* and *decrescendi*, as the old Italians used to do, and as *all Germans* do who have learned anything.

SECTION XXXV

HOW TO HOLD ONE'S SELF WHEN PRACTISING

In practising the singer should always stand, if possible, before a large mirror, in order to be able to watch himself closely. He should stand upright, quietly but not stiffly, and avoid everything that looks like restlessness. The hands should hang quietly, or rest lightly on something, without taking part in the interpretation of the expression. The first thing needed is to bring the body under control, that is, to remain quiet, so that later, in singing, the singer can do everything intentionally.

The pupil must always stand in such a way that the teacher can watch his face, as well as his whole body. Continual movements of the fingers, hands, or feet are not permissible.

The body must serve the singer's purposes freely and must acquire no bad habits. The singer's self-possession is reflected in a feeling of satisfaction on the part of the listener. The quieter the singer or artist, the more significant is every expression he gives; the fewer motions he makes, the more importance they have. So he can scarcely be quiet enough. Only there must be a certain accent of expression in this quietude, which cannot be represented by indifference. The quietude of the artist is a reassurance for the public, for it can come only from the certainty of power and the full command of his task through study and preparation and perfect knowledge of the work to be presented. An artist whose art is based on power cannot appear other than self-possessed and certain of himself. An evident uneasiness is always inartistic, and hence does not belong where art is to be embodied. All dependence upon tricks of habit creates nervousness and lack of flexibility.

Therefore the singer must accustom himself to quietude in practising, and make his will master of his whole body, that later he may have free command of all his movements and means of expression.

The constant playing of single tones or chords on the piano by the teacher during the lesson is wrong, and every pupil should request its discontinuance. The teacher can hear the pupil, but the latter cannot hear himself, when this is done; and yet it is of the utmost importance that he should learn to hear himself. I am almost driven distracted when teachers bring me their pupils, and drum on the piano as if possessed while they sing. Pupils have the same effect on me when they sit and play a dozen chords to one long note.

Do they sit in the evening when they sing in a concert?

Do they hear themselves, when they do this? Unfortunately, I cannot hear them.

Poor pupils!

It is enough for a musical person to strike a single note on the piano when he practises alone, or perhaps a common chord, after which the body and hands should return to their quiet natural position. Only in a standing posture can a free deep breath be drawn, and mind and body be properly prepared for the exercise or the song to follow.

It is also well for pupils to form sentences with the proper number of syllables upon which to sing their exercises, so that even such exercises shall gradually gain a certain amount of expressiveness. Thus the exercises will form pictures which must be connected with the play of the features, as well as with an inner feeling, and thus will not become desultory and soulless and given over to indifference. Of course not till the mere tone itself is brought under complete control, and uncertainty is no longer possible, can the horizon of the pupil be thus widened without danger.

Only when a scene requires that a vocal

passage be sung kneeling or sitting must
the singer practise it in his room long
before the performance and at all rehearsals,
in accordance with dramatic requirements
of the situation. *Otherwise the singer should
always* STAND. We must also look out for
unaccustomed garments that may be required
on the stage, and rehearse in them; for instance, hat, helmet, hood, cloak, etc. Without becoming accustomed to them by practice,
the singer may easily make himself ridiculous on the stage. Hence comes the ab-
surdity of a Lohengrin who cannot sing
with a helmet, another who cannot with a
shield, a third who cannot with gauntlets;
a Wanderer who cannot with the big hat,
another who cannot with the spear, a Jose
who cannot with the helmet, etc. All these
things must be practised before a mirror
until the requirements of a part or its cos-
tume become a habit. To attain this, the
singer must be completely master of his body
and all his movements.

It must be precisely the same with the voice. The singer must be quite independent of bad habits in order consciously to exact from it what the proper interpretation of the work to be performed requires.

He should practise only so long as can be done without weariness. After every exercise he should take a rest, to be fresh for the next one. After the great scale he should rest *at least* ten minutes; and these resting times must be observed as long as one sings.

Long-continued exertion should not be exacted of the voice at first; even if the effects of it are not immediately felt, a damage is done in some way. In this matter pupils themselves are chiefly at fault, because they cannot get enough, as long as they take pleasure in it.

For this reason it is insane folly to try to sing important rôles on the stage after one or two years of study; it may perhaps be endured for one or two years without evil results, but it can never be carried on indefinitely.

Agents and managers commit a crime when they demand enormous exertions of such young singers. The rehearsals, which are held in abominably bad air, the late hours, the irregular life that is occasioned by rehearsals, the strain of standing around for five or six hours in a theatre, — all this is not for untrained young persons. No woman of less than twenty-four years should sing soubrette parts, none of less than twenty-eight years second parts, and none of less than thirty-five years dramatic parts; that is early enough. By that time proper preparation can be made, and in voice and person something can be offered worth while. And our fraternity must realize this sooner or later. In that way, too, they will learn more and be able to do more, and fewer sins will be committed against the art of song by the incompetent.

SECTION XXXVI

CONCERNING EXPRESSION

WHEN we wish to study a rôle or a song, we have first to master the intellectual content of the work. Not till we have made ourselves a clear picture of the whole should we proceed to elaborate the details, through which, however, the impression of the whole should never be allowed to suffer. The complete picture should always shine out through all. If it is too much broken into details, it becomes a thing of shreds and patches.

So petty accessories must be avoided, that the larger outline of the whole picture shall not suffer. The complete picture must ever claim the chief interest; details should not distract attention from it. In art, subordination of the parts to the whole is an art of itself.   Everything must be fitted to the larger lineaments that should characterize a masterpiece.

A word is an idea; and not only the idea, but how that idea in color and connection is related to the whole, must be expressed. Therein is the fearsome magic that Wagner has exercised upon me and upon all others, that draws us to him and lets none escape its spell.   That is why the elaboration of Wagner's creations seems so much worth while to the artist.   Every elaboration of a work of art demands the sacrifice of some part of the artist's ego, for he must mingle the feelings set before him for portrayal with his own in his interpretation, and thus, so to speak, lay bare his very self.   But since we must impersonate human beings, we may not spare ourselves, but throw ourselves into our task with the devotion of all our powers.

SECTION XXXVII

BEFORE THE PUBLIC

IN the wide reaches of the theatre it is needful to give an exaggeration to the expression, which in the concert hall, where the forms of society rule, must be entirely abandoned. And yet the picture must be presented by the artist to the public from the very first word, the very first note; the mood must be felt in advance. This depends partly upon the bearing of the singer and the expression of countenance he has during the prelude, whereby interest in what is coming is aroused and is directed upon the music as well as upon the poem.

The picture is complete in itself; I have only to vivify its colors during the performance. Upon the management of the body, upon the electric current which should flow between the artist and the public, — a current that often streams forth at his very appearance, but often is not to be established at all, — depend the glow and effectiveness of the color which we impress upon our picture.

No artist should be beguiled by this into giving forth more than artistic propriety permits, either to enhance the enthusiasm or to intensify the mood; for the electric connection cannot be forced. Often a tranquillizing feeling is very soon manifest on both sides, the effect of which is quite as great, even though less stimulating. Often, too, a calm, still understanding between singer and public exercises a fascination upon both, that can only be attained through a complete devotion to the task in hand, and renunciation of any attempt to gain noisy applause.

To me it is a matter of indifference whether the public goes frantic or listens quietly and reflectively, for I give out only what I have undertaken to. If I have put my individuality, my powers, my love for the work, into

a rôle or a song that is applauded by the
public, I decline all thanks for it to myself
personally, and consider the applause as belonging to the master whose work I am interpreting. If I have succeeded in making him
intelligible to the public, the reward therefor
is contained in that fact itself, and I ask for
nothing more.

Of what is implied in the intelligent interpretation of a work of art, as to talent and
study, the public has no conception. Only
they can understand it whose lives have been
devoted to the same ideals. The lasting understanding of such, or even of a part of the
public, is worth more than all the storm of
applause that is given to so many.

All the applause in the world cannot repay
me for the sacrifices I have made for art, and
no applause in the world is able to beguile me
from the dissatisfaction I feel over the failure
of a single tone or attempted expression.

What seems to me bad, because I demand
the greatest things of myself, is, to be sure,

good enough for many others. I am, however, not of their opinion. In any matter relating to art, only the best is good enough for any public. If the public is uncultivated, one must make it know the best, must educate it, must teach it to understand the best. A naïve understanding is often most strongly exhibited by the uncultivated — that is, the unspoiled — public, and often is worth more than any cultivation. The cultivated public should be willing to accept only the best; it should ruthlessly condemn the bad and the mediocre.

It is the artist's task, through offering his best and most carefully prepared achievements, to educate the public, to ennoble it; and he should carry out his mission without being influenced by bad standards of taste.

The public, on the other hand, should consider art, not as a matter of fashion, or as an opportunity to display its clothes, but should feel it as a true and profound enjoyment, and do everything to second the artist's efforts.

Arriving late at the opera or in the concert hall is a kind of bad manners which cannot be sufficiently censured. In the same way, going out before the end, at unfitting times, and the use of fans in such a way as to disturb artists and those sitting near, should be avoided by cultivated people. Artists who are concentrating their whole nature upon realizing an ideal, which they wish to interpret with the most perfect expression, should not be disturbed or disquieted.

On the other hand, operatic performances, and concerts especially, should be limited in duration and in the number of pieces presented. It is better to offer the public a single symphony or a short list of songs or pianoforte pieces, which it can listen to with attention and really absorb, than to provide two or three hours of difficult music that neither the public can listen to with sufficient attention nor the artist perform with sufficient concentration.

SECTION XXXVIII

INTERPRETATION

LET us return to the subject of Expression, and examine a song; for example,

"*Der Nussbaum*," *by Schumann.*

The prevailing mood through it is one of quiet gayety, consequently one demanding a pleasant expression of countenance. The song picture must rustle by us like a fairy story. The picture shows us the fragrant nut tree putting forth its leaves in the spring; under it a maiden lost in reverie, who finally falls asleep, happy in her thoughts. All is youth and fragrance, a charming little picture, whose colors must harmonize. None of them should stand out from the frame. Only one single word rises above the rustling of the tree, and this must be brought plainly to the hearing of the listening maiden

— and hence, also, of the public — the second
"*next*" year. The whole song finds its point
in that one word. The nut tree before the
house puts forth its green leaves and sheds
its fragrance; its blossoms are lovingly em-
braced by the soft breezes, whispering to each
other two by two, and offer their heads to be
kissed, nodding and bowing; the song must
be sung with an equal fragrance, each musical phrase in one breath : that is, with six
inaudible breathings, without ritenuto.

They whisper of a maiden who night and
day is thinking, she knows not of what herself. Between " selber" and " nicht was "
a slight separation of the words can be made,
by breaking off the *r* in " selber" nasally;
and holding the tone nasally, without taking
a fresh breath, attacking the " nicht" anew.
In this way an expression of uncertainty is
lent to the words " nicht was."

But now all becomes quite mysterious.
" They whisper, they whisper" — one must
bend one's thoughts to hear it; who can

understand so soft a song? But now I hear plainly, even though it be very soft — the whisper about the bridegroom and the next year, and again quite significantly, the *next* year. That is so full of promise, one can scarcely tear one's self away from the thoughts, from the word in which love is imparted, and yet that, too, comes to an end!

Now I am the maiden herself who listens, smiling in happiness, to the rustling of the tree, leaning her head against its trunk, full of longing fancies as she sinks to sleep and to dream, from which she would wish never to awaken.

"Feldeinsamkeit" by Brahms.

This song interprets the exalted mood of the soul of the man who, lying at rest in the long grass, watches the clouds float by, and whose being is made one with nature as he does so. A whole world of insects buzzes about him, the air shimmers in the bright sunlight, flowers shed their perfume; everything about him lives a murmuring life in tones that seem to enhance the peace of nature, far from the haunts of men.

As tranquil as are the clouds that pass by, as peaceful as is the mood of nature, as luxurious as are the flowers that spread their fragrance, so tranquil and calm must be the breathing of the singer, which draws the long phrases of the song over the chords of the accompaniment, and brings before us in words and tones the picture of the warm peace of summer in nature, and the radiant being of a man dissolved within it.

I mark the breathing places with V. " Ich liege still im Nohen grünen Gras V und sende lange meinen Blick V nach oben V [and again comfortably, calmly] nach oben.

"Von Grillen rings umschwärmt V ohn' Unterlass V von Himmelsbläue wundersam umwoben V von Himmelsbläue V *wundersam umwoben.*"

Each tone, each letter, is connected closely with the preceding and following; the expression of the eyes and of the soul should be

appropriate to that of the glorified peace of
nature and of the soul's happiness. The last
phrase should soar tenderly, saturated with a
warm and soulful coloring.

" Die schönen weissen Wolken zieh'n dahin
V durch's *tiefe* Blau *V*, [I gaze at it for a
moment] wie schöne, stille Träume *V* [losing
one's self] wie schöne stille Träume. *V*
[A feeling of dissolution takes away every
thought of living and being.] Mir ist *V* als ob
V ich längst *V* gestorben bin! [The whole
being is dissolved in the ether; the end comes
with outstretched wings soaring above the
earth.] und ziehe selig mit *V* durch ew'ge
Räume *V* und ziehe selig mit *V* durch ew'ge
Räume. [Dissolution of the soul in the uni-
verse must sound forth from the singer's
tone.]

" *The Erlking*," *by Schubert.*

For him who is familiar with our native
legends and tales, the willows and alders in
the fields and by the brooks are peopled with
hidden beings, fairies, and witches. They

stretch out ghostly arms, as their veils wave over their loose hair, they bow, cower, raise themselves, become as big as giants or as little as dwarfs. They seem to lie in wait for the weak, to fill them with fright.

The father, however, who rides with his child through the night and the wind, is a man, no ghost; and his faithful steed, that carries both, no phantom. The picture is presented to us vividly; we can follow the group for long. The feeling is of haste, but not of ghostliness. The prelude should consequently sound simply fast, but not overdrawn. The first phrases of the singer should be connected with it as a plain narrative.

Suddenly the child hugs the father more closely and buries his face in terror in his bosom. Lovingly the father bends over him; *quietly* he asks him the cause of his fear.

Frightened, the child looks to one side, and asks, in disconnected phrases, whether his

father does not see the Erlking, the Erlking
with his crown and train.   They had just rid-
den by a clump of willows.   Still quietly, the
father explains *smilingly* to his son that what
he saw was a bank of fog hanging over the
meadow.

But in the boy's brain the Erlking has
already raised his enticing whisper.[1]   The
still, small voice, as though coming from
another world, promises the child golden
raiment, flowers, and games.

Fearfully he asks his father if he does not
hear the Erlking's whispered promises.

"It is only the dry leaves rustling in the
wind."   The father quiets him, and his voice

[1] The voice of the Erlking is a continuous, soft, uninterrupted stream of tone, upon which the whispered words
are hung.   The Erlking excites the thoughts of the fever-
sick boy.   The three enticements must be sung very rapidly,
without any interruption of the breath.   The first I sing as
far as possible in one breath (if I am not hampered by the
accompanist), or at most in two; the second in two, the
third in three; and here for the first time the words "reizt"
and "brauch ich Gewalt" emerge from the whispered
pianissimo.

is full of firm and loving reassurance, but he feels that his child is sick.

For but a few seconds all is still; then the voice comes back again. In a low whisper sounds and words are distinguished. Erlking invites the boy to play with his daughters, who shall dance with him and rock him and sing to him.

In the heat of fever the boy implores his father to look for the Erlking's daughters. The father sees only an old gray willow; but his voice is no longer calm. Anxiety for his sick child makes his manly tones break; the comforting words contain already a longing for the journey's end — quickly, quickly, must he reach it.

Erlking has now completely filled the feverish fancy of the child. With ruthless power he possesses himself of the boy — all opposition is vain — the silver cord is loosened. Once more he cries out in fear to his father, then his eyes are closed. The man, beside himself, strains every nerve — his own

and his horse's; his haste is like a wild flight.
The journey's end is reached; breathless they
stop — but the race was in vain.

A cold shudder runs through even the
narrator; his whole being is strained and
tense, he must force his mouth to utter the
last words.

SECTION XXXIX

IN CONCLUSION

THE class of voice is dependent upon the inborn characteristics of the vocal organs. But the development of the voice and all else that appertains to the art of song, can, providing talent is not lacking, be learned through industry and energy.

If every singer cannot become a *famous* artist, every singer is at least in duty bound to have learned something worth while, and to do his best according to his powers, as soon as he has to appear before any public. As an artist, he should not afford this public merely a cheap amusement, but should acquaint it with the most perfect embodiments of that art whose sole task properly is to ennoble the taste of mankind, and to bestow happiness; to raise it above the miseries of

this workaday world, withdraw it from them,
to idealize even the hateful things in human
nature which it may have to represent, without departing from truth.

But what is the attitude of artists toward
these tasks?

CLEVELAND, January 11, 1902.

NOTE

A Good Remedy for Catarrh and Hoarseness

Pour boiling hot water into a saucer, and let a large sponge suck it all up. Then squeeze it firmly out again. Hold the sponge to the nose and mouth, and breathe alternately through the nose and mouth, in and out.

I sing my exercises, the great scale, passages, etc., and all the vowels into it, and so force the hot steam to act upon the lungs, bronchial tubes, and especially on the mucous membranes, while I am breathing in and out through the sponge. After this has been kept up for ten or fifteen minutes, wash the face in cold water. This can be repeated four to six times a day. The sponge should not be full of water, but must be quite squeezed out. This has helped me greatly, and I can recommend it highly. It can do no injury because it is natural. But after breathing in the hot steam, do not go out immediately into the cold air.